Lanson Boyer

From the Orient to the Occident

Or, L. Boyer's Trip across the Rocky Mountains, in April, 1877

Lanson Boyer

From the Orient to the Occident
Or, L. Boyer's Trip across the Rocky Mountains, in April, 1877

ISBN/EAN: 9783337149123

Printed in Europe, USA, Canada, Australia, Japan

Cover: Foto ©Andreas Hilbeck / pixelio.de

More available books at **www.hansebooks.com**

FROM THE

ORIENT TO THE OCCIDENT,

OR

L. BOYER'S TRIP ACROSS THE ROCKY MOUNTAINS,

IN APRIL, 1877.

———◆•◆———

New York:

E. WELLS SACKETT & BRO., LAW, BOOK AND JOB PRINTERS,

CORNER PINE AND WILLIAM STREETS.

1878.

THIS VOLUME IS DEDICATED

TO

MY WIFE,

AS A

TOKEN OF LOVE AND RESPECT.

"A WORD TO THE READER."

DEAR FRIENDS : Let me disarm criticism beforehand by assuring you that no person could point out a failure or a shortcoming in this little book, which I do not know all about and deplore.   In fact, I have my doubts as to calling it a book at all.   No, let me rather say, that this book of mine is a vehicle through which, with a longing for sympathy, I convey to you my pleasure, annoyances and experiences in the journey it narrates ; or, if you like it better, it is a casket enshrining the memory of many a pleasant hour made bright and indelible by your companionship, your kindness, your attention and hospitality. Take then, these recollections, dear friends, and each one of you find among these lines something worthy of respect; and, for you, *O critic!* if you will indeed attempt to find fault with what is written, remember that in all courtesy you should deal gently and generously with a work proclaiming itself from the outset not so much a book as long gossipy lectures to one's friends, and an amicable attempt to convey to them some of the delights it commemorates.   And if you do not find a great deal in it, *dear critic,* remember that to competently judge of these lectures one must have learned to read between the lines and find there the pith and the memory of the whole.

LANSON BOYER.

FROM THE ORIENT TO THE OCCIDENT,

OR

L. BOYER'S TRIP ACROSS THE ROCKY MOUNTAINS.

IN APRIL. 1877.

———•———

To the Members of Atlantic Lodge No. 50, I. O. O. F.

BROTHERS : On the third day of April my family, with a lady friend (Mrs. W. Gregory) and myself, started on a western trip.

We took the cars at Jersey City for Washington, and arrived there the next morning, and at 8.40 A. M., April 4th, we started for Louisville, Ky., on the Baltimore and Ohio Railroad. We followed up the Potomac Valley and River, the most crooked I ever saw. We passed through Harper's Ferry, where John Brown went up to glory, as his spirit marches along to the tune of Glory Hallelujah. We saw the house he was captured in, and a tumble-down looking old building it is.

During the trip up this valley we passed a place called the Deer Park, a summer residence of Gov. Morgan of Pennsylvania. It is a very handsome place, and a great resort for hunting deer. The mode of hunting them is as follows : The hunters cut notches in the trees and fill them with salt. The deer come to eat the salt, and then go to a river near by, called the Cheat River, to drink, and while in the act are shot by the hunters.

Snow and plowing was often seen from the car window. Along the Potomac Valley the railroad often runs on very high places in the mountains. Many times the track leads over precipices 500 feet high—dreary, wild-looking places indeed. Often we were over 3,000 feet high.

The next morning (April 5th) we arrived at Cincinnati, but could not spare time to see the city. It is too well known, however, to need any description by me. It is the great pork depot of our nation. The city proper is built on a high hill, and runs down to the Ohio River, on the opposite bank of which is Covington, a pretty town in Kentucky. At seven o'clock we started on our tour to the Mammoth Cave in Kentucky, via Louisville. We arrived at Cave City at seven P. M. We were obliged to take stage for the cave, some nine miles distant, over a rocky, mountainous country. On going up the mountain side we broke down—one wheel gave out. There we were, in the midst of a dreary waste of rocks, trees, and mountains, broken down, and about sunset at that. The prospect was nót very flattering—no house or even a barn to gladden our sight. We had four horses; concluded to take two horses, go back down the mountain to Cave City, and get another stage. The passengers would have to pass away the time as best they might. This was done, and late in the evening we arrived at the cave, tired, hungry, and cross. April 6th, at about eight o'clock in the morning, we entered the cave, and remained until late in the afternoon, when we returned to the hotel, very much pleased and satisfied with that we had seen; but as I have not the power or even the wit of a ready writer, you will excuse me if I do not make myself properly understood, but I will to the best of my ability undertake to give here some idea of what we saw on this occasion. In the first place, I am told it exceeds anything of the kind in the world. I do not know this to be a fact, but I am ready to believe any and all stories that may be told about this wonderful cave. Photographs of the cave can be seen at my office by any brother who chooses to call.

Our guide tells us there are over one hundred miles of avenues and roads in this cave. We came to a river called the Echo River, which was so high it could not be crossed. A curious thing about this river is there are fish without eyes in it. I have one at my office in a vial, and it can be seen at any time by any brother. There is a river on the surface of the earth near by called the Green River, and when the Green River rises Echo River rises also, and when one river is low the other one is low also. For this reason it is supposed there is a hidden connection between the two. This supposition, however, is and will remain an unsolved mystery. The entrance to the cave is 194 feet above the Green River, 30 feet in width, over which may be seen at all seasons of the year a mist or fog when the temperature of the outer air suits.

The Mammoth Cave breathes once in a year; that is to say, in the summer the current sets from the cave, and in the winter it sets inward. The average temperature of the cave is 59 degrees the year round. On entering the cave, for a few hundred yards in summer, when the temperature is one hundred degrees, the air rushes out with such force as to extinguish a lighted lamp. Passing into the cave, however, for about half a mile, the motion of air is barely perceptible at any time, from the fact that the main avenue enlarges so rapidly that it plays the part of a reservoir, when a current of air from any direction is speedily neutralized. Thus you will see that a change of seasons is unknown in the Mammoth Cave; therefore day or night, morning or evening, has no existence in this wonderful place. In fact, there is an eternal sameness here, the like of which has no parallel. In many portions of the cave bats in untold numbers are seen sticking to the rocks overhead, and if you go near enough to them with your light or lamp (for each one of us have a lamp), they will be found sticking to the rock with their hind feet, head downwards, and making a noise similar to that made by mice, and if you undertake to tear or drive one of them off, you have a job on hand, for they will bite and strike with their wings. A comical looking "*bird*" they are, and must be seen to be appreciated.

The inner air of the cave differs greatly with the outer air. Many persons, on coming out of the cave, find it exceedingly difficult to breathe for a few moments. The air inside the cave is so pure that, emerging from the cave, the air outside is found to be insufferable—so much so as to be offensive to the smell, which quickly dispells the romance of a pure country air. You might ask what kind of diseases would be benefited there. Well, consumptives at one time visited the cave, and with partial results. Some died there, and all of them died when exposed to the external air. One man remained in the cave over five months, and did not see the light once during that time; he was brought out dead. Short trips are attended with good results, but a cave residence is fatal. Short and easy trips have been known to effect a cure in chronic diarrhea when all other kinds of treatment failed. The stone in which this wonderful chasm is carved out is limestone. Stalactites are seen on every hand. They are formed by drops of water dropping down from the ceiling or roof of the cave. These droppings of water are from limestone, and if the stone is white, the stalactites will be transparent; but if the stone contains black oxide of iron, they will be red or yellowstone color. Stalactites are found by these drops of water forming on the floor of the cave, and often those from above and below form a junction almost midway, and by placing a lamp on one side you can see quite plainly through them. Saltpetre was made in large quantities in 1812-14 by nitrate of lime and soda and carbonate of potash, of which large quantities were found in the cave, and a number of the old vats or tubs that were used at that time are still in good repair, and with a little trouble saltpetre can be furnished in large quantities again.

After leaving a small archway near the mouth of the cave, called the Narrows. you enter the main cave, and it is six miles long, and varies from 40 to 100 feet in height, and from 60 to 300 feet in width. The rotunda is entered on leaving the Narrows The ceiling is 150 feet high and 175 feet in diameter; the floor is strewed with remnants of vats, water pipes, wood, and other materials used in making saltpetre in 1812.

To the right of the rotunda a cave called Audobon's Avenue leads off for half a mile, to a collection of stalactites, and during the winter millions of bats live here, and a hissing noise is heard from them continually. Some fifteen years ago a number of small stone cottages were built by consumptive people for the purpose of residing here during their sickness. They were told by their physicians that that kind of treatment would be expected in curing them. Some thirteen had their cottages in this dark and dismal cave. Three of them died here, and the rest, when appearing again on the surface, lived from three days to three weeks.

Those who remained in the cave three or four months presented a frightful appearance; their faces externally bloodless, eyes sunken, and pupils dilated to such a degree that the iris ceased to be visible, so that no matter what the color of the eye was originally, it soon appeared all black.

We leave the rotunda, and pass over the high cliffs to the left; they are hanging cliffs indeed, and are called the Methodist Church, 80 feet in diameter and 40 feet high; here forms the pulpit, which consists of a ledge of rocks 25 feet in height. The Gospel was preached here from this pulpit 40 years ago; the logs or benches occupy the same position which they did when first placed in the Church. We pass from the rotunda to the Grand Arch, which is 50 feet high, and 60 feet wide. To the left of the path, leading to the giant's coffin, are found two immense rocks, many tons in weight fallen from the roof above, and are standing in upright positions; the giant's coffin is a large rock, 40 feet long and 20 feet wide, and 8 feet deep, and at the point from where it is viewed it presents a striking resemblance to an immense coffin. On the ceiling, to the left of the giant's coffin, is a picture of an Ant-Eater, natural as life, formed by the droopings of black gypsum on the ceiling. A little fur ther on the ceiling is presented a group of figures called the giant, wife and child ; the giant is in the act of passing the child to the giantess. Still further on a colossal elephant may be observed on the ceiling.

From the giant's cave to the mouth of the Mammoth Cave wheel tracks and the impression of feet can be very distinctly seen, which were made nearly 50 years ago ; at that time the earth was moist and soft. but now the whole ground is as hard as adamant.

We next come to the Star Chamber, situated in the main cave, 60 feet high, 70 feet wide, and 500 feet long ; the ceiling is composed of black gypsum, and is studded with innumerable white points, and by dimlight they present a most striking resemblance to stars, and when the guide takes his lamp and descends below, or behind a ledge of rocks, by which a cloud is made to pass slowly over the ceiling, it is difficult to divest oneself of the idea that a storm is approaching, and it needs but the flash of lightning and the roar of thunder to make the illusion complete; after producing the storm illusion, the guide disappears with all the lamps through a lower arch-way, hundreds of yards in length, leaving the visitor in total darkness ; the guide appears at the extreme end of the arch-way, holding in advance of him all the lamps ; as he slowly elevates the lights from the cavern from which he rises, it produces the illusion of the rising sun ; with the exception of Echo River, the Star Chamber is the most attractive object in the cave.

The floating cloud room connects the Star Chamber with Proctor's Arcade.

Proctor's Arcade is the most magnificent natural Tunnel in the world, 100 feet in width, 45 feet in height, and a mile in length ; the ceiling is smooth, the walls are upright, and look as though they had been chiseled out of solid rock ; when this Arcade is lighted up at the western terminus with Bengal Lights, the view is magnificent beyond description.

We next come to a rotunda 400 feet in diameter, the ceiling is 40 feet high and perfectly level, and the wonder is that the ceiling has strength to sustain itself, for the surveyor says it is not more than forty feet from the surface of the earth.

The cave at this point is very dry, and no change of any kind is taking place in it, otherwise there might be some danger of the ceiling falling in.

When this immense area is illuminated at both ends, as it is by the guides, it presents a most magnificent appearance. At the eastern extremity of this rotunda is a column extending from the floor to the ceiling, called the Nicholas Monument, named after one of the guides who has been in the cave as such for over 36 years.

A short distance beyond the rotunda, the main Cave leads off several avenues or branches, the one to the left leads off to the black chamber, which is 100 feet wide and 20 feet high, the walls and ceiling covered with a black substance ; this is the most gloomy room in the cave.

The avenues lead off to the right, one communicates with the fairy grotto, which contains a most magnificent collection of stalactites, and this avenue is one mile in length ; the other avenue communicates with a solitary cave, at the entrance of which there is a small cascade. The Cliff City is in the main cave, beyond the rocky pass, and is 100 feet in diameter, and 40 feet in height, the floor is covered with pieces of rock, and they present the ruins of an ancient city. We next come to the long route ; the visitor leaves the main cave, at the foot of the giant's coffin, and passes into the deserted chamber ; the distance from the mouth of the cave to the maelstrom situated at the end of the long route, is 9 miles.

We next come to the Wooden Bowl, and it receives its name from the fact that a wooden bowl, such as used by the Indians in early times, was found in it when first discovered, and the cavern is in the shape of a wooden bowl.

Martha's Palace is entered by passing a steep declivity and a pair of steps, called the Steps of Time, and this
palace is 40 x 60 feet.

Side-Saddle Pit, over which there rests a dome, is
reached by passing through what is called the arch-way,
all bearing evidence of water running through it; this
pit is 90 feet deep and 20 feet across.

The bottomless pit looms up as we leave the side-saddle pit, it is 175 feet deep and 40 feet wide, and a bridge
has been thrown across it, from which this pit may be
viewed with safety; right over this pit is a dome, called
Shelby's dome. 60 feet high, and 40 feet in diameter; pit
and dome reaching the distance of 235 feet right up and
down.

As you leave the bottomless pit you enter a room 20
feet in height, and 40 feet in diameter, and at this place
it is the custom for visitors to have a rest and refresh the
inner-man with food, brought by the guides, for by this
time we are all very hungry, and the way we eat would
astonish the Cannibal Islanders.

We next come to a place called the Scotchman's Trap,
a low arch-way, called the Valley of Humility, the ceiling
of which is smooth and white, and appears as though it
had been plastered; this low archway runs along for a
mile or more, and finally descends down a stairway leading to Echo River. The story of the Scotchman's Trap,
is peculiar, and it runs something like this: a Scotchman
was visiting the cave, and when he came to this long,
lone, narrow passage-way, he refused to advance any further, the guides were at their wits end, for the best part
of the cave was further on, and it would never do to stop
right here, the guides recollected a passage-way from the
narrow gang-way leading into the bottomless pit, from
which a person could be hauled up with ropes into the
main avenue, although it had never been used before by
them, a distance of some 235 feet, and to convince the old
Scotchman of the feasibility of this, to him a hazardous
attempt, they undertook the job among themselves, it

proved a grand success, and the Scotchman was satisfied and went on his journey rejoicing, and from that time until now it has been called the Scotchman's Trap.

A short distance from the old Scochman's Trap is placed a very curious shaped rock. called the Shanghae Chicken, from a forced resemblance to that beautiful bird.

The next avenue we come to is the Fat Man's Misery ; it is a narrow avenue, 150 feet in length, and looks as if it had been cut out of the solid rock by the action of running water. This avenue varies from a foot and a half to three feet wide ; the upper part from 4 to 10 feet high, and contrary to all calculations, there never was a man too large to pass through Fat Man's Misery.

Great Relief is entered on leaving Fatman's Misery, and it varies from 40 to 60 feet in width, and 20 feet in hight. From the ceiling great limestones hang, and they appear to be ready to fall on the heads of visitors at any time should a sudden shake give them a chance.

The traces of the water that once passed through this avenue could be very easily seen in the lines of gravel, sand and mud, now laying on the floor. We now come to River Hall, extending from Great Relief to the River Styx, which is about 60 feet in width.

Bacon Chamber comes next, and it receives its name from the fact that small pieces of rock, hanging from the ceiling, resemble very much Bacon Hams.

The next is the " Dead Sea." This is a body of water 15 feet deep and 50 feet in length, and 40 feet below the terrace that leads to the natural bridge. This Sea was discovered when the cave was, by passing over the Terrace, which was attended with great danger. We next come to the Lake, called the Lake Leathe, 500 feet long by 40 feet wide, and from three to thirty feet deep ; the ceiling over the Lake is 90 feet high. Visitors, in taking the Long Route, cross this lake in boats. After crossing Lake Leathe we strike the great walk leading to Echo River, a distance of 1,500 feet ; the ceiling is 40 feet high,

and the floor is covered with yellow sand. We now come
to Echo River, and it is reached from Great Walk to Silliman's Avenue, and almost a mile long. The Avenue
leading to the river, at its entrance, is about three feet
high; but immediately beyond the point of entrance it
spreads out some 15 feet high, and varies in width from
20 to 200 feet, and in depth from 10 to 30 feet. When
there is no rise in Green River, which is on the surface
of the earth, the water in Echo River becomes very clear,
so much so that rocks can be seen 20 feet below the surface, and the boat appears to be gliding through the air.
The connection between Echo and Green River is near the
commencement of Silliman's Avenue. When Green River
is rising, Echo River runs in the direction of Great Walk.
When Green River falls, the current in Echo River runs
in the opposite direction. The temperature of the place
is always 59 degrees, and where the water from Green
River runs into Echo River, at a temperatare higher than
that of the Cave, a dense fog is produced, not inferior to
the fogs of Newfoundland, and inexperienced persons
have been known to get lost in the fog. A rise of 18 feet
of water in Echo River cuts off all communication with
the outer world. Among the great curiosities of this
river are the Eyeless Fish. These fish are perfectly
white.

As we progress in our journey, we come to Silliman's
Avenue, a mile and-a-half long, and extending from Echo
River to El Ghor, varying in height from 20 feet to 40
feet, in width from 20 to 200 feet. The walls of this Avenue are ragged and water-worn, and there is no doubt of
its recent formation, compared with the other parts of the
cave. The objects of interest in this Avenue, are as follows :

1st. "Cascade Hall," 200 feet in diameter and 20 feet high,
and derives its name from a small cascade, which falls
from the ceiling and the Avenue that leads to " Roaring River," and takes its origin in Cascade Hall.

2d. Dipping Spring," a pool of water supplied from the ceiling. Stalactites and staglamites are found at this place in great numbers.

3d. The "Infernal Regions, which receive its name from the fact that the floor is composed of wet clay, and it is almost impossible to pass over it without slipping down.

4th. The "Sea Serpent," is a crevice in the rock overhead, cut in by running water, and presenting very much the appearance of a great serpent.

5th. The "Valley Wayside," is a small avenue leading off from Silliman's Avenue, and returning into it a short distance further on.

6th. "The Great Western," which is a large rock, many times larger than any vessel ever built, and the end of it closely resembles the stern of a ship.

8th. "The Rabbits," a large stone resembling very much that animal.

9th. "Ole Bull Concert Room," 30 feet wide and 20 feet high, not a very big building to hold a concert in; but when Ole Bull first visited the cave he held a concert here, and hence the name "Ole Bull Concert Room."

10th. "Silliman's Avenue," named after Professor B. Silliman, of Yale College.

Rhodas Arcade arises in Silliman's Avenue, and is 1,500 feet long and 10 feet high. The walls and ceiling are covered with crystals and carbonate of lime of indiscribable beauty, and in that respect there is no avenue superior to it.

You reach Lucy's Dome by passing through Rhodas Arcade, 60 feet in diameter and over 300 feet high, being the highest dome in the cave. The sides have the appearance of immense curtains reaching from the ceiling to the floor.

The next in order is the pass of El Ghor, resembling Silliman's Avenue, and about two miles in length.

1st. The Hanging Rocks, and they look as if in the act of falling ; but none have since the discovery of the cave.

2d. The Fly Chamber, so called from the fact that crystals of black gypsum, of the size of a house fly, project from the ceiling in great numbers.

3d. The Table Rock, 20 feet long, and projecting from the left side of the avenue 10 feet, and about two feet in thickness.

4h. "The Crown," 6 feet in diameter, about 10 feet from the floor, and resembling very much the object after which it was named.

5th. Boone's Avenue leads off to the left, and has been explored for about half a mile ; but nothing beyond is known as to its extent or dimensions.

6th. Corrunes Dome, rests directly over the centre of the avenue, and is very beautiful.

7th. The Black Hall of Calcutta is on the left side of the Avenue, and about 15 feet deep.

8th. Stella's Dome, which is reached by passing through a small avenue which enters the left wall of the pass.

9th. The Chimes, consist of hanging rocks, and, when struck, send forth a musical sound like a chime of bells.

10th. Wellington Gallery, is not very attractive, although taking up quite a space in the cave.

11th. Hebe Spring is about 4 feet in diameter and $2\frac{1}{2}$ feet deep, and charged with sulphur. Fifteen years ago there was no sulphur perceptible, and even now, when it has not been disturbed for many hours, pure water may be dipped from its surface, and sulphur water from the bottom, indicating that this spring is supplied with two kinds of water, pure at the top and sulphurous at the bottom.

12th. Eyeless Crowfish are found in the spring.

13th. A half mile beyond Hebe's Spring, the pass to the El Ghor communicates with a body of water, the extent of which is unknown, and it is called Mystic River.

Next we come to Martha's Vineyard, 20 feet above the pass of El Ghor, and reached by a ladder near Hebe's Spring. The walls and ceiling are studded with stalactites of carburette of lime, and colored with black oxyd of iron, which in size and appearance resemble grapes. A large stalactite projects from the right wall, and is called the Battering Ram.

We now come to Washington Hall and Snow-Ball room. Washington Hall is 60 feet wide, 20 feet high and 100 feet long. The visitors reach this point about noon, and this place is selected as the Dining Hall. Cans of oil are kept here to replenish our lamps, which hold oil enough for ten hours, but are replenished every five hours.

The Snow-Ball room is between Washington Hall and Cleveland Avenue, and the ceiling is studded with white gypsum, looking for the world like snow balls.

Now we come to Cleveland Avenue, 1¾ miles in length, 60 feet wide and 20 feet high. The walls and ceiling of this avenue are literally lined with alabaster forms of every conceivable variety and beauty. On entering Cleveland Avenue the objects of special interest present themselves in the following order :

1st. Mary's Bower, 15 feet high.

2d. The Cross, made from two crevices in the rock overhead, at right angles, and lined with flowers of Plaster of Paris. The cross is 8 feet in length.

3rd. The Memory Ceiling.

4th. The Last Rose of Summer, 8 inches in diameter and of snowy whiteness.

5th. The Dining Table, 15 feet wide and 30 feet long.

6th. Bacchus' Glory, an alcove 3 feet in height and 5 feet long, and lined with grapes of gypsum.

7th. St. Ceilla's Grotto, remarkable for the size of stucco flowers to be found in it.

8th. Diamond Grotto is lined with crystals of selinite, and when a light is moved before them they sparkle like diamonds ; hence the name.

9th. Charlotte's Grotto, the terminus of Cleveland's Avenue.

10th. Cleveland's Avenue is named in honor of Professor Cleveland, the distinguished mineralogist.

Rocky Mountains come next, and they are rocks fallen from above, and on the top of the mountain is a stalagmite 2 feet high and 6 inches in diameter, termed Cleopatra's Needle. On the far side of the Rocky Mountains is a gorge 70 feet deep, termed Dismal Hollow. The cave at the mountain divides into three branches: the one to the right leads to sandstone, and is near the surface of the earth ; the one to the left runs to Grogham's Hall ; the one in the centre to Franklin Avenue.

Grogham's Hall constitutes the end of the long route and is 70 feet wide and 20 feet high ; the left wall is covered with stalactites, transparent in color and of great hardness, which are made into ornaments of various kinds.

The Maelstrom is a pit 175 feet deep and 20 feet wide. There are avenues running from the bottom, which may be seen when a light is lowered down into the pit, but they have never been fully explored.

A peculiar kind of rat has been found in Grogham's Hall, and has eyes resembling those of a rabbit. The hair is like the gray squirrel's, but the legs are white. Cave crickets and lizzards are found here also. The cave cricket is an inch long, body yellow, striped with black, provided with large eyes, sluggish in their movements, and, unlike other crickets, they never make a noise. The cave lizzard is from three to five inches in length, eyes prominent, body yellow and dotted with black spots, and they are semi-transparent, and sluggish in their movements. The attendance of animal life in this part of the cave indicates that there is communication with the surface of the earth at no great distance. Bats are found in all parts of the Cave.

We are now at the Gothic Arcade, which is found by

ascending a flight of steps 15 feet in height. The objects of note are:

1st. The Seat of the Mummy, a niche in the wall just large enough for a person to sit in. The body found in this niche was that of an Indian female, dressed in the skins of animals and ornamented with the trinkets belonging to the Indian. A few feet distant was the body of a child, attired in a similar manner, discovered resting against the wall. Both in a good state of preservation. No doubt they wandered into the cave, and, getting lost, sat down and died in the same position in which they were found.

On one occasion, a gentleman wandered from his party, and by some accident his lamp went out; and endeavoring to escape, he became alarmed, and finally insane, when, crawling behind a rock, he remained in that position 48 hours; and although the guides passed the rock a number of times, he did not make the slightest noise, and, when finally discovered, he tried to make his escape, but was too much exhausted to run.

A lady allowed her party to get so far ahead that their voices could not be heard, and in attempting to overtake them, fell and extinguished her lamp, when she became terribly frightened, swooned, and when discovered in a short time afterward she had lost her mind, and did not recover for many years afterward.

Not a year passes but the guides are obliged to search for persons who have been foolhardy enough to leave their party, and who, in every instance, became speedily bewildered, and when found were crying bitterly or saying their prayers. In such cases the guides are overpowered with kisses, embraces and other demonstrations of gratitude.

The proper course for a person to pursue who becomes lost in the Cave is to remain in the place where they first became confused, and not to stir until rescued by the guides. They will not have to remain more than from three to ten hours from the time they should have returned to the hotel.

The objects of interest in Gothic Arcade are as follows:

1st. A short distance from the Seat of the Mummy is a large stalactite, extending from the floor to the ceiling, called the Post Oak, and resembles the oak tree growing in the neighborhood.

2d. The First Echo, the floor of which, when struck with some heavy metallic weight, emits a hollow sound.

3rd. The Register Room is 300 feet long, 40 feet wide and 16 feet high. In this room hundreds of persons have displayed very ill-taste in tracing on the white walls their names with the smoke of the lamps or candles.

4th. Gothic Hall, a large room, the ceiling sustained by enormous columns, which, lighted by our lamps, present a beautiful appearance.

5th. Vulcan's Smithy, resembling a blacksmith's forge.

6th. Bancroft's Breastwork consists of a ledge of rocks detached from the side of the avenue, against which they stand.

7th. The Arm Chair is formed by the union of stalactites and stalagmites, forming a beautiful seat like a chair.

8th. The Elephant's Head, a large stalagmite projecting from the floor, resembling an elephant's head very much.

9th. Lover's Leap consists of a rock projecting 15 feet over a pit 70 feet deep.

10th. Gatewood's Dining Table is a flat rock detached from the ceiling, 12 feet long and 8 feet wide, and is named after one of the saltpetre miners.

11th. Napoleon Dome is 50 feet high and 30 feet wide.

12th. Lake Purity is a pool of perfectly transparent water, situated directly under Vulcan's Smithy. The next in order is the Labyrinth and Gorham's Dome. The Labyrinth is entered from the deserted chamber by descending a pair of stairs. A figure of an American eagle is plainly seen upon the wall.

Gorham's Dome is reached by passing over a bridge and then ascending a ladder in the Labyrinth. You see this dome from a natural window half way between the floor and ceiling of the dome. It is 200 feet high and 60 feet wide. When the far end of the dome is reached, a Bengal light is inserted in it, and the view is sublime. Avenues connect with the top and bottom of this dome. Gorham's Dome bears the name of its discoverer.

We now come to Pensacola Avenue, which is a mile in lenth, 60 feet in height, and 100 feet wide, and the following are the principal objects worthy of examination :

1st. The Sea Turtle, 30 feet in diameter ; a rock fallen from the ceiling and resembling a sea turtle.

2d. The Wild Hall, in size and appearance, resembles a bandit's hall.

3rd. Snow Ball receives its name by the appearance of points in the wall, looking like snow balls.

4th. The Great Crossing is a point where four great avenues commence.

5th. Mat's Arcade, 150 feet long, 30 feet wide and 60 feet high. Also a beautiful collection of stalactites called the Pineapple Bush.

I will mention in conclusion that there are 150 avenues in this cave—some have been explored, and others have not and are never entered by visitors—which I have not attempted to describe. The total length of all the avenues is over 100 miles. And now, brothers, I could mention many other avenues in this cave, and very interesting they would be ; but without wearying your patience, I will resume my journey west.

On April 7th, we left the cave in a stage for Cave City, about nine miles, to take the cars. We went down the mountain in good order. No broken bones or detentions. In the cars again, and bound for Louisville, and at 7 P. M., we arrived there, and went to Louisville Hotel, and a pleasant place to stop in it is, too. The next day (Sunday) it rained all day. No church for our little party, but kept our rooms writing down our travels, sending

letters home, and resting from the fatigue of the day previous, when in the cave ; for we now began to feel the
efforts made during our visit to the cave.

At about noon the next day, April 9, we again took the
cars of the Ohio and Mississippi Railroad—a very
straight road, running through many miles of prairie
land, cut up into large farms, and under good cultivation,
especially in the State of Illinois. It has rained all day,
and the streams are very much swollen. The bridges on
the road have to be watched closely, as the country is
flooded everywhere. The farmers are very much dis-
couraged, as they are trying to finish up their spring
work and planting.

We are to-day, while it rains very hard outside, taking
our comfort and ease in our drawing-room car. We are
shut out from all other passengers, and spend the time
reading, telling stories, singing (for we have a splendid
singer with us, Mrs. W. Gregory), or looking out
the window at the sights as they pass along, and
truly we could not enjoy ourselves any better if we
were in our own parlors at home. At 9 P.M., we crossed
that great river of rivers, the Mississippi, over that great
iron tubular bridge at St. Louis, the greatest piece of
engineering skill to be found anywhere in the world. It
has a history familiar to most of us, but had I the time
I would give you some of the particulars of its construction. I will mention one fact only : the original estimate
of the cost was $4,000,000, but when finished it cost
$13,000,000.

On entering St. Louis the cars pass through a tunnel,
and come out on the other side of the city, and then enter
a large depot, and at 9:40 P.M. we are ready to start for
Omaha ; but our little company, feeling very tired,
wanted to stay at Louisville over night, and go to the
Southern Hotel, and in the morning start on our journey
again. My idea was to pass on that night, and thus gain
so much time. It finally ended in our going on that
night, and we arrived at Omaha the next morning. The

first thing I heard the next morning was an "Extra" out, giving a description of the burning of the Southern Hotel, at St. Louis, and many lives were lost. I bought the paper, rushed up to our rooms, and read the news to our little party, and I can say, Brothers, for a time there was weeping among us for joy, to think of what a calamity we had all escaped ; for when guests remain only a short time (especially if the hotel is full) they are invariably given rooms on the top floors, and those who read of this terrible accident will remember that the guests on the upper floors fared the worst.

After that there was no backing or filling, each one to have his or her way, but it was decided to do just as I said. Now to return. We took the train for Omaha, arrived safe, and went to the Grand Central Hotel, and next morning took seats in one of the most magnificent trains of cars made up by any railroad in the United States. Everything is first-class. Pullman sleeping coaches are attached to this train, and all travelers know how finely they are furnished, and how they tend to relieve the wearisome monotony of tedious days in the journey from ocean to ocean. At this depot we find all the waiting-rooms, ticket-offices, baggage-rooms, lunch-stands, news and book-stands, together with one of the best-kept eating-houses in the country, with books and papers to while away our leisure hours. We are finally ready for a start. The bell rings ; the whistle shrieks, and off we go. We have one of the rooms in the Pullman coach all to ourselves, and we are shut out from all intruders, and as we are by ourselves, we are, as if at home, enjoying ourselves as we travel westward.

The first thing of notice is the streams of water running in every direction ; at least it appears so from the windows of our car, the country being very level, that every declivity or elevation of the earth will turn a stream.

The White River and the Wabash River are the two large rivers first passed going over the plains. The houses are small and mostly thatch work. It is wonderful to see the level plains ; miles and miles of prairie land are passed ; no trees of any kind are seen for many miles.

We are now passing through a lovely prairie land, mostly tilled by farmers from the East.

We do not see any fences for many miles. They have a day out here called *"Arbur Day,"* and on that day all persons who have charge of farms and land stop all work and plant young trees from early morn until late at night, and among the farmers this day is kept by seeing who can plant the greatest number of trees. The Government pays a certain bounty for the greatest number of trees planted on that day by any one person, and this day is held on the 18th of April in each year.

We next come to the Platte River, a large stream running through the Platte Valley. This valley is about twenty miles wide, and is owned by the Union Pacific Railroad ; for this company own twenty miles of land on either side of the track, which they sell to farmers and others.

We are to-day passing through the grasshopper country, and the farmers here are much troubled about this destroying insect, many of them are over *nine inches long*, and are ferocious looking indeed : and I have the boss of them preserved in a bottle, in liquor, for exhibition. He is the commander of the grasshopper brigade

out West, and the story runs that he, with his army, after
cleaning out all the grain fields in the neighborhood, took
the next express train for another section of the country.
While in transit the *Herald* newsboy came along through
the cars selling the paper ; the *Grasshopper Boss* bought
a copy, and looking over the news found this item—saying
that the grasshoppers had migrated to parts unknown,
but they had left one field, belonging to a poor man, un-
touched. The boss felt mad ; laid down the paper ; put
his spectacles in his pocket ; pulled the bell-rope, and
stopped the train; ordered off his brigade, and took the
next express train back to the poor man's farm ; and I,
at a great expense, collected an army of *wild western
turkey gobblers;* met this advancing host of grasshoppers ; charged upon mine enemy ; destroyed them ; saved
the poor man's wheat-field, and captured the boss himself ; had him preserved in whisky ; ordered him (by express) home, and I have the animal here to-night on
exhibition. Ladies and friends please examine him. Is
he not all that I represent him to be ?

As I look out of our window, I behold numerous
prairies on fire, for the country is very dry and dusty,
and the prairie grass burns very easily, and during the
first night's ride westward from Omaha, we gaze out of
our car windows at the great prairies seen all around us.

These prairies, which in the day time seemed dry, dull
and uninteresting, gave place at night to the lurid play
of the fire fiend, and the heavens and the horizon seem
like a furnace.

A prairie on fire is a fearfully exciting and fear-in-
spiring sight ; cheeks blanche as the wind sweeps its
volume toward the observer, and as the train comes near
the flames, leap higher and higher, and the smoke forms
a dark background, from which is reflected the fire's
brilliantly-tinged light.

Far out on the prairies, beyond the settlements, the
fires rage unchecked for miles and miles, but nearer to
the little settlement, where the cabin has been set up, it is

the deadliest foe and most dreaded enemy of the settler. No words can describe ; no pencil paint the look of terror when he beholds advancing toward him the fire fiend; for, while he is unprepared and unprotected, when the first sign of fire is given, all hands turn out. Either a counter fire is started, which, eating from the little settler's ranche, in the face of the wind, toward the grand coming volume, takes away its force, and stops its progress by leaving it nothing to feed on, or else furrows are broken with a plow around the settler's home. The cool earth is then thrown up, and all the grass beyond is fired, while the house enclosed within is safe. These fires create a strong current, or breeze, by their own heat, and often advance at the rate of twenty miles an hour or more, and the terrible lurid light by night, and the blackened path left behind, as seen the next day by the traveler, are sights never to be forgotten.

I have been rather long in describing to you prairie fires, but I thought the subject needed it, and, therefore, you will please excuse the time taken.

Friday, April 12th.—We are still passing over the Nebraska plains, and are now in the alkali plains. The water here is not fit to drink, being impregnated very much with lime. On either side we behold myriads of cattle feeding on the prairie grass. A Mr. Iliff, who lives near by, owns over 40,000 head of cattle, and has a ranch over 150 miles for them to graze on. We are passing through his land now, and we behold cattle on either side of us as far as the eye can reach.

It does not often rain here, and they have had little or no rain for the past fifteen months, and everything looks dry and parched; but the farmers say they do not want any rain now until the Fall. Cattle are now feeding on hay, drying on the plains, which rain would spoil to such an extent the cattle would refuse to eat it and starve in consequence.

Very often we pass small streams of water, and around these streams stock most do congregate.

We have now passed through the first snow shed, at an elevation of some 6,000 feet. Our train is drawn by two powerful locomotives. In one day we have ascended nearly 5,000 feet. We are also passing through snow drifts, many of them over seven feet deep.

After leaving the great cattle ranch, we come to the great Platte Valley, from a place called Fremont. This valley is from five to fifteen miles wide, and, before the railroad was built, was the great highway for overland travel to the far West. Leaving the Mississippi River at different points, the emigrants' route would lead through this valley.

The luxurious grasses near the water of the Platte River made this a favorite route. This valley has also been the scene of many deadly conflicts with "Lo, the poor Indian," and many an emigrant lies buried beneath some rough and hastily made mound near the roadway, minus his scalp, or his bones lie bleaching in the sun at noonday.

But a wonderful change took place when the railroad was run through this place. The "bull whacker," with his white-covered wagon and rawboned oxen, his slang phrases and profane expressions, his rough life, and, in many instances, his violent death, the crack of his long lash, that would ring out in the clear morning air like a rifle, and his wicked goad ox-prong, an instrument of torture to his beasts; I say all this has passed away, their glory has departed, and in their place the snorting engine and the thundering train.

· Through this valley are many farm houses, surrounded with the cotton wood tree, similar to our poplar tree. These trees have been planted by the farmer in the last six or eight years, and their growth is enormous. Trees sixty feet high and eight to ten inches thick are no uncommon result of a six or eight years' growth.

One of the finest sights for an Eastern traveler is to see Platte Valley in the Spring or early Summer, and the farmer from the East is more than surprised to see such a beautiful valley, all ready to receive the seed without any preparation other than the breaking of the ground; no stumps, no stones, no underbrush or anything to prevent him from going right to work on his farm.

Platte Valley must be seen to be appreciated. Only a few years ago it was hardly tenanted by any one but the dirty redskins; to-day the farmer strides over their broad sides, monarch of all he surveys. But there is ample room for many more yet to come, and the land can be bought from the Union Pacific Railroad at from three to ten dollars per acre. .

I will give you a description of one farmer on the Platte Valley, who came from one of the Eastern States with very little cash. He bought his farm from the rail-road company in 1867, and up to 1874, seven years, he cultivated, in wheat and corn, on an average 130 acres. His receipts from these two crops in seven years were $13,314; his expenses $4,959, leaving a net increase of $8,355, besides increase in the value of the land, fully $2,000 more; and this was done on a capital of less than $2,000 at the beginning. The winds, which blow mostly from the west, are very constant and often very high, making shelter of great importance to stock and fruit trees; hence the importance of planting trees around the house and barns ; and, as I told you a few moments ago, these farmers devote, at certain seasons of the year, much time to the planting of trees, and the rapidity of growth in the rich soil reminds one of the growth of trees and fruit in the South. Walnut trees, in eight years, have measured 22 inches around and 30 feet high. Maple trees, 12 years' growth, have measured 43 inches round four feet from the ground, and white willow 45 inches round of twelve years' growth.

I mentioned the immense number of cattle seen on these plains. The question is asked, how does an owner know his own stock. '

Well, they have ranches at certain places, a plot of

land fenced in, and a one-story thatched roof cottage put up inside for the use of the rangers or herders, as they are called.

I have been in some of them, and I say here to-night, that any farmer in this section of the country has his hog pen in a more respectable condition than these cottages out West, intended for people to live in.

These rangers or herders are men who have charge of a herd of cattle, and one herder, with his mustang, can take care of many thousand head of cattle. These cattle take care of themselves. Once a year the cattle on the plains are driven into the ranches; then they are branded by the herders on the right hind hip with a burning iron into the flesh the first letter of the surname of the owner. They are then let loose again to hunt food for themselves, until the time comes to ship them off to market, which happens as often as the owner is in want of money.

These herders are a peculiar kind of people. I will
• describe them: With long hair and beard, wide-rimmed hats (Buffalo Bill style), the best fitting boots that money can buy, long spurs jingling at their heels, a small arsenal of Colt's revolvers and Bowie knives strapped to their waist, and their chief pleasure is to be in a row. Their chief drink is whisky straight, and they usually seem to feel better when they have killed somebody. Houses of prostitution, gin mills and gambling hells follow in their wake.

They are generous to their friends and revengeful to their enemies. Human life is of but little account with them. Their life is one of continued exposure and very laborious. They are perfect horsemen, usually in the saddle 16 hours out of every 24, and their great ambition is to become a "devil of a fellow." Nor does it require much on their part to fill the bill. Thousands of them on the plains have died with their boots on, and we suppose thousands more will perish the same way. Living violent lives, of course they meet with violent deaths. They are a peculiar people, answering a peculiar end, for almost 99 out of every 100 go down to the vile dust from whence they sprung, unkempt, unhonored and unsung.

The crops of this valley are various. Splendid crops of wheat, corn, oats, barley, broom corn, potatoes, cabbages and onions are raised in great quantities during variable seasons, but raising stock is the most sure pay in the long run, for Horace Greeley says (in his life), that it costs no more to raise a cow on the prairies than a chicken here, and I believe the philosopher was right.

In our travels we came to a town called Plum Creek, named after a creek on the other side of the Platte River. The town is the center of a number of stage routes running into the surrounding country and the mines.

There was a battle fought with the Indians during the building of the railroad here in 1867 through this town, by a band of "Cheyenne," under a chief called "Turkey Leg." This same beautiful "Lo" now draws his rations and whisky straight from Uncle Sam, at the Red Cloud Agency. This Turkey Leg is a vicious looking fellow, and his appearance naturally suggests a hanging bee at the next lamp-post. I watched this develish-looking beast up and down the platform for some time, so much so that he noticed it. He then goes and whispers to another beautiful "Lo," and pointing to me, he made a demonstration very significant about taking off my scalp. I took my hat off, bowed very low, and this fiend incarnate looked at me with the utmost contempt, and I heard something like this coming from him: "A dam big lie, no scalp."

I will relate to you an account of the fight that this beautiful "Lo" was chief in, and it is as follows:

"While the railroad was being built, the engineers, graders and tracklayers were frequently driven from their work by the Indians. Not only then but after the track was laid and trains running. It was sometimes torn up and trains ditched, causing loss of lives and destruction of property. One of these attacks took place near Plum

Creek, as we will now relate : In July, 1867, a train was ditched about four miles west of the above named station. It was by a band of Southern Cheyennes, under a chief called Turkey Leg, who now draws his rations regularly from Uncle Sam, at the Red Cloud Agency. He is a vicious looking fellow, his appearance naturally suggesting him as a fit subject for a hanging bee. At a small bridge, or culvert, over a dry ravine, they had lifted the iron rails from their chairs on the ties—raising only one end of each rail—about three feet, piling up ties under them for support, and firmly lashing the ties and rails together by wire cut from the adjoining telegraph line. They were pretty cunning in this arrangement of the rails, and evidently placed them where they thought they would penetrate the cylinder on each side of the engine, but not having a mechanical turn of mind exactly, and disregarding the slight curve in the road at this point, they missed their calculation, as the sequel shows, as one of the rails did no execution whatever and the other went straight into and through the boiler. After they had fixed the rails in the manner described, they retired to where the bench or second bottom slopes down to the first, and there concealed themselves in the tall grass waiting for the train. Before it left Plum Creek, a hand car, with three section men, was sent ahead as a pilot. This car encountered the obstacle and entered the ravine, bruising and stunning the men and frightening them so that they were unable to signal to the approaching train. As soon as the car landed at the bottom of the ravine, the Indians rushed up, when two of the men, least hurt, ran away in the darkness of the night—it was a little past midnight—and hid in the tall grass near by. The other, more stunned by the fall of the car, was scalped by the savages, and as the knife of the savage passed under his scalp he seemed to realize his condition partly, and, in his delerium, widly threw his arms out and snatched the scalp from the Indian who had just lifted it from his scull. With this he, too, got

away in the darkness, and he is now an employee of the
Company at Omaha. But the fated train came on with
out any knowledge of what had transpired in front. As
the engine approached the ravine, the head-light gleam-
ing out in the darkness in the dim distance, fast growing
less and less, the engineer, Brooks Bowers by name, but
familiarly called 'Bully Brooks" by the railroad men,
saw that the rails were misplaced, whistled 'down
brakes,' and reversed his engine, but all too late to stop
the train. The door of the fire box was open and the
fireman was in the act of adding fuel to the flames
within when the crash came. That fireman was named
Hendershot, and the boys used to speak of him as the
'Drummer Boy of the Rappahannock,' as he bore the
same name and might have been the same person whose
heroic deeds, in connection with Burnside's attack on
Fredericksburg, are now matters of history. He was
thrown against the fire-box, when the ravine was reached,
and literally roasted alive; nothing but a few of his
bones being afterwards found. The engineer was thrown
over the lever he was holding in his hands. through the
window of his cab, some twenty feet or more. In his
flight the lever caught and ripped open his abdomen,
and when found he was sitting on the ground holding his
protruding bowels in his hands. Next to the engine
were two flat cars loaded with brick ; these were landed,
brick and all, some thirty or forty feet in front of the
engine, while the box cars, loaded with freight, were
thrown upon the engine and around the wreck in great
disorder ; after a time these took fire and added horror
to the scene. The savages now swarmed around the
train and whooped and yelled in great glee. When the
shock first came, however, the conductor ran ahead on
the north side of the track to the engine, and there saw
Bowers and Hendershot in the position we have described
them. He told them he must leave them and flag the
second section of the train following after, or it, too,
would be wrecked. He then ran back, signaled this

train, and with it returned to Plum Creek. Arriving
there in the middle of the night, in vain did he try to get
a force of men to proceed at once to the scene of the disaster. No one would go. In the morning, however,
they ralied, armed themselves and went out to the wreck,
By this time it was near 10 o'clock ; the burning box-cars
had fallen around the brave engineer, and while the fiery
brands had undoubtedly added to his agony, they had also
ended his earthly existence. His blackened and charred
remains only told of his suffering. The rescuing party
found the train still burning ; the Indians had obtained all
the plunder they could carry and left in the early morning.
In the first gray dawn of the morning they manifested
their delight over the burning train in every possible
way, and their savage glee knew no bounds. From the
cars not then burned, they rolled out boxes and bales of
merchandize, from which they took colored flannels,
calicos and other fancy goods. Bolts of these goods they
would loosen and with one end tied to their ponies' tails,
or the horn of their saddles, they would mount and start
at full gallop up and down the prairie just to see the
bright colors streaming in the wind behind them. But
the end of this affair was not yet ; the avenging hand of
justice was on the track of these blood-thirsty villains,
who, for some inscrutable reason, are permitted to wear
the human form. In the Spring of that year, by order
of Gen. Augur, then in command of the military depart-
ment of the Platte, Major Frank North, of Columbus,
Neb., who had had no little experience in the business, was
authorized to raise a batallion of two hundred Pawnee
Indians, who were peaceable and friendly towards the
whites, and whose reservation is near Columbus, for
scouting duty. It was the old experiment of fighting
the devil with fire to be tried over again.

The scouts were to fight the various hostile bands of
the Sioux, Arrapahoes, and Cheyennes, and assist in
guarding the railroad and the railroad builders. At the
time this train was attacked, these scouts were scattered

in small detachments along the line of the road between
Sidney and the Laramie plains. General Augur was
immediately notified of it, and he telegraphed Major
North to take the nearest company of his scouts and
repair as soon as possible to the scene of the disaster.
At that time Major North was about fourteen miles west
of Sidney, at the end of the track, and his nearest company was some twelve miles further on. Mounting his
horse, he rode to their camp in about fifty minutes, got
his men together, and leaving orders for the wagons to
follow, returned, arriving at the end of the track about
4 o'clock in the afternoon. By the time these men and
horses were loaded on the cars, the wagons had arrived,
and by 5 o'clock the train pulled out. Arriving at Jules-
burg they were attached to a passenger train, and by
midnight, or within twenty-four hours after the disaster
took place, he arrived at the scene. Meanwhile other
white troops, stationed near-by, had arrived. In the
morning he was ordered by General Augur to follow the
trail and ascertain whether the attack had been made by
Northern or Southern Indians. With ten men he
started on the scout. The sharp-sighted Pawnees soon
struck the trail. They found where the hostile band had
crossed the river, and where they had abandoned some
of their plunder. They followed the trail all day, and
found that it bore south to the Republican Valley. From
this fact, and other indications that only Indians would
notice, he ascertained that the attacking band were
Southern Cheyennes. Returning from this scout, after
about thirty-five miles travel, he reported to the commanding officer at Omaha, and received orders to remain
in the vicinity and thoroughly scout the country, the
belief being generally entertained among the officers that,
if not followed, the Indians would soon return on another
raid. Subsequent events proved this belief to be true,
and they had not long to wait. In about ten days, their
camp being at Plum Creek, one of the scouts came running into camp from the bluffs south of Plum Creek, and
reported that the Indians were coming.

He had discovered them in the distance, making their
way in the direction of the old overland stage station,
which they soon after reached. Arriving here, they un-
saddled their horses and turned them loose in an old
sod corral to feed and rest. They then began prepar-
ations to remain all night. The scouts, however, proposed to find out who and what they were before evening
approached. Major North first determined to go with
the company himself, but, at the urgent solicitation of
Captain James Murie, finally gave him charge of the
expedition. There were in the command two white com-
missioned officers—Lieut. Isaac Davis, besides the Captain—two white servants, and forty-eight Pawnees. The
company marched from their camp straight south to the
Platte River. which they crossed ; then turning to the
left, followed down its bank, under the bushes, to within
a mile and a half of the creek. Here they were discovered
by the Cheyennes. Then there was mounting in hot
haste—the Cheyennes at once preparing for the fray.

There were one hundred and fifty warriors to be pitted
against this small band of fifty-two, all told. But the
Cheyennes, up to this time, supposed they were to fight
white soldiers, and were very confident of victory. Forming in regular line, on they rushed to the conflict. Captain Murie's command, as soon as they found they were
discovered, left the bushes on the river bank and went
up into the road, where they formed in line of battle
and were ordered to charge. As the order was given, the
Pawnees set up their war-whoop, slapped their breasts
with their hands, and shouted " Pawnees !" The oppos-
ing lines met on the banks of the creek, through which
the scouts charged with all their speed. The Cheyennes
immediately broke and fled in great confusion, every man
for himself. Then followed the chase, the killing, and
the scalping. The Indians took their old trail for the
Republican Valley, and put their horses to the utmost
speed to escape the deadly fire of the Pawnees. Night
finally ended the chase, and when the spoils were

gathered, it was found that fifteen Cheyenne warriors had been made to bite the dust, and their scalps had been taken as trophys of victory. Two prisoners were also taken; one a boy of about sixteen years, and the other a squaw. The boy was a nephew of Turkey Leg, the chief. Thirty-five horses and mules were also taken, while not a man of the scouts was hurt. After the chase had ceased, a rain-storm set in, and, tired with their day's work, with the trophies of their victory they returned to camp. It was about midnight when they arrived. Major North and a company of infantry, under command of Captain John A. Miller, had remained in camp, guarding government and company property, and knowing that a battle had been fought, were intensely anxious to learn the result. When the Pawnees came near, it was with shouts and whoops and songs of victory. They exhibited their scalps and paraded their prisoners with great joy, and spent the whole night in scalp dances and wild revelry. This victory put an end to attacks on railroad trains by the Cheyennes. The boy and squaw were kept in the camp of the Pawnees until late in the season, when a big council was held with the Brule Sioux, Spotted Tail's band, at North Platte, to make a new treaty.

Hearing of this council, Turkey Leg, Chief of the Cheyennes, sent in a runner and offered to deliver up six white captives held in his band for the return of the boy and the squaw. After the necessary preliminaries had been effected, the runner was told to bring the white captives, that the exchange might be made. The boy held by the scouts was understood to be of royal lineage, and was expected to succeed Turkey Leg in the chieftaincy of the tribe.

After the exchange had taken place, the old chief would scarcely allow the boy to leave his sight, such was his attachment to him, and manifested his delight in every possible way over his recovery. The white captives were two sisters by the name of Thompson, who lived south of the Platte River, nearly opposite Grand Island, and their twin brothers; a Norwegian girl, taken on the Little Blue River, and a white child born to one of these women while in captivity. They were restored to their friends as soon as possible.

THE NEXT ATTACK.—The Indians were not willing to have the iron rails that should bind the shores of the continent together laid in peace, and made strenuous and persistent efforts to prevent it. On the 16th of April, 1868, a " cut off" band of Sioux, under a scalawag chief, named " Two Strikes," attacked and killed five section-men near Elm Creek station, taking their scalps, and ran off a few heard of stock. They were never pursued. On the same day, and evidently according to a pre-arranged plan, a part of the same band attacked the post at Sidney. They came up on the bluffs north of the town, and fired into it. But no one was injured from their shooting at that time. Two conductors, however, named Tom Cahoon and William Edmunson, had gone down to the Lodge Pole Creek, a little way, to fish. They were unobserved by the Indians when the firing took place. Hearing the reports they climed up the bank to see what was going on, and being seen by the Indians, they at once made an effort to cut them off, though they were only a mile or so from the post. The savages charged down upon them and shot Cahoon, who fell forward on the ground. The Indians immediately scalped him and left him for dead. Mr. Edmunson ran towards the post as fast as he could, and drawing a small Derringer pistol fired at his pursuers. Thinking he had a revolver, and would be likely to shoot again if they came too close, they did not venture up as they had done, but allowed him to escape. He got away with some eight or nine arrow and bullet wounds together, and carrying four arrows sticking in his body. He was taken to the hospital, and rapidly recovered from his wounds. After the Indians had gone, the citizens went after the body of Mr. Cahoon, whom they supposed dead, but to their surprise he was still alive. They brought him into the post, where he recovered, and is now running on the road.

ATTACK AT OGALALLA.—In September of the same year the same band of Sioux attempted to destroy a train between Alkali and Ogalalla. They fixed the rails the same as at Plum Creek. As the train came up the rails penetrated the cylinders on each side of the engine, as it was a straight track there, the engine going over into the ditch, with the cars piling on top of it. The engineer and one of the brakemen, who was on the engine at the time, were thrown through the window of the cab, and were but little hurt. The fireman was fastened by the tender against the end of the boiler, and after the train had stopped, there being no draft, the flames of the fire came out of the door to the fire-box upon him, and the poor fellow was literally roasted alive. He was released after six hours in this terrible position, during which he begged the attendants to kill him, but lived only a few moments after his release. All the trains at this time carried arms, and the conductor, with two or three passengers, among whom was Father Ryan a Catholic priest of Columbus, Nebraska, seized the arms and defended the train, the Indians meanwhile skulking among the bluffs near the track, and occasionally firing a shot. Word was sent to North Platte, and an engine and men came up, who cleared the wreck. Meanwhile word was sent to Major North, then at Willow Island, to take one company of his scouts and follow the Indians. He came to Alkali and reported to Colonel Mizner, who was marching from North Platte with two companies of cavalry, all of whom started in pursuit.

They went over to the North Platte River, crossed that stream, and entered the sand-hills, where the scouts overtook and killed two of the Indians; the whole party going about thirty-five miles, to a little lake, where the main body of the Indians had just left, and camped, finding the smouldering embers of the Indian fires still alive.

That night some of the white soldiers let their camp

fires get away into the prairie, and an immense prairie fire was the result. This, of course, alarmed the Indians, and further pursuit was abandoned, much to the disgust of the scouts. Colonel Mizner also claimed that his rations were running short; but from all the facts we can learn, he lacked the disposition to pursue and capture those Indians. At least this is a charitable construction to put upon his acts.

The Indians have made some efforts to ditch a few trains since that year, but have effected no serious damage. Their efforts of late have mostly been confined to stock stealing, and they are never so happy as when they have succeeded in running off a large number of horses and mules. When the road was first built it was their habit to cross it going south and north several times in each year. They roamed with the buffaloes over the plains of Nebraska, Colorado, Wyoming, and Kansas. The effort of the Government of late has been to confine them on their own reservations, and the rapid disappearance of the buffaloes from the regions named have given them no excuse for hunting in the country now crossed by railroads and filling up with settlers.

Indians pray as well as other people. I will repeat a prayer by the Indian to the Great Spirit:

"I am a poor Indian that is bad. Make me a chief; " give me plenty of horses; give me fine clothing. I ask " for good spotted horses; give me a large tent; give me " a great many horses; let me steal fine horses; grant it " to me. Give me guns by cheating. Give me a beauti- " ful woman. ' Bring the buffalo close by. No deep " snow; a little snow is good. Give me Black Feet to " kill—close by, all together. Stop the people from " dying; it is good. Give instruments for amusement; " blankets too, and fine meats to eat. Give the people " altogether plenty of fine buffalo and plenty to eat."

We have been running for many hours through a country where "stock-raising" is the principal business done; where cattle and horses can grow and are kept the year round* without being housed, but live their lives on the prairies, eating prairie grass, which is a rich nutriment that produces fat and renders cattle ready for the market without feeding them grain.

Over these plains also the Grand Duke Alexis had his first buffalo hunt. This hunt was gotten up by some of the Indians stopping in this valley, and who, at a few moments' warning, are always ready to gamble, to drink, or to have a war-dance or a fight on the plains. These beautiful "Los" (Indians, by a better name) went in company with the Grand Duke and Buffalo Bill, the hunter and actor, Generals Sheridan and Custer (since deceased: killed in a fight with these same Indians). These red devils appeared in a pow-wow and a war-dance to astonish the Grand Duke before they started on the hunt. Not long after, they spied a buffalo, and went for him, the Grand Duke ahead, who had a very fleet horse, and soon caught up with the buffalo, the monster of the plains, and coming in proper range he fired his big pistol and shot the buffalo dead at his feet. The next thing for the Grand Duke to do was to canter off to a telegraph station and telegraph home to his father, the Czar of all the Russias, that he had killed the first wild, horned monster that had met his eye in America. This sport continued for two days, and ended in a series of Indian festivities.

We now come to North Platte, another division of the Union Pacific Railroad, and 291 miles from Omaha. This town has abundant attractions for the invalid needing rest, with antelope and deer in the mountains, fish in the streams and an abundance of pure air to invigorate the body.

Near-by here is a singular structure of rock, called the Chimney Rock. Some years ago it was over 500 feet high and situated in the plains, with no other rock near it. It could be seen for many miles around. In fact, it was the guiding-mark for weary travelers on their trip out West. But the elements are reducing its size and height, until now it is not nearly as large or high as it was some years ago.

All along here can be seen evidences of old battles fought with the Indians.

We now come to where prairie dogs can be seen from the car windows as we pass along. Ladies clap their hands, and children shout with glee, at sight of these funny little creatures. It is a curious little animal in shape, always fat, gray in color, about 16 inches in length, and always lives with a multitude of its companions in villages. It has a short, yelping bark, which it is very fond of uttering, and it is something like the bark of a puppy. In the same hole with the prairie dog is found the gray owl, and often you will see the owl on one side of the hole and the prairie dog on the other. The rattlesnake is often found there, too. Truly a happy family : the owl, the prairie dog and the rattlesnake. The question was asked me, How do the prairie dogs get water to drink ? On inquiring, I find they dig their own wells, each village of dogs having one well, with a concealed opening. It matters not how far down the water may be, the dogs will keep digging until they reach it. A well of over 200 feet deep has been found, and there is a circular stairway leading down to the water. Every time a prairie dog wants a drink he descends this staircase, which, considering the great distance, is no mean task.

In our travels, we come across the bullwhacker again. Some time ago I gave a partial description of this individual, but will once more trespass upon his premises, and, with your permission, will proceed. He is a very large man, very strong, with long, unkempt hair and the stiffest of beards. Eight or ten yoke of oxen are usually attached to a wagon, by the side of which hangs the trusty rifle or ax. Of the bullwhacker, it is said that his oath and his whip are both the longest ever known. The handle of his whip is not over three feet long ; the lash, however, is seldom less than twenty feet, from the stock to the tip. This tip is called the persuader, and under its influence the ox team will progress at the rate of twenty miles a day. The effect on a lazy ox is wonful, and when he feels the lash on his flank, it will cause him to double up, as if seared with a red-hot iron. The bullwhacker is considered the champion swearer of America, and can drink more whisky than any other kind of man. He is astonishingly accurate in his aim with the lash. One of his favorite pastimes is to cut with his lash a coin from the top of a stick stuck in the ground.

A Bullwhacker bet with a comrade that he could cut out of his pantaloons, on the back side, a piece of the size of a sixpence ; the stake was a pint of whiskey ; the Bullwhacker lost if he cut the skin. The comrade stooped over so as to give the Bullwhacker a good chance, the blow was given carefully, but in earnest, when the tallest jump ever put on record was made ; the comrade was minus a portion of his skin, as well as a large fragment of his breeches, and the Bullwhacker called out "thunder and lightning, I've lost the whiskey."

We next come to a town by the name of Sidney, 414 miles from Omaha, and here we get a good supper ; the house is kept by J. B. Rumsey, and a good meal is sure to be had.

There is a charm in life on the great prairies, to one who is going over them for the first time, it seems lonely indeed, and yet it is never wearisome ; now comes great rolling uplands of enormous sweep, sometimes the grand distances are broken by rugged butts and bluffs ; as they arise in sight the traveler is as eager in his curiosity as the sea voyager is to catch the first sight of distant shore.

The plains are covered most of the time with natural flowers ; the sun flower is most preferred, and can be seen for many miles. Wherever the Railroad or wagon route has made its way across the country there springs up the ever living sun flower. The plains are also covered with tufts of shrubbery, called sage brush, they are from

six inches to three feet high, and there is another variety
called "greasewood," about the same kind of wood as
the sage brush.

Agriculture is certain as far West as 300 miles from the
Mississippi River, beyond that to the mountains no crops
can be seen.

We are now at Cheyenne, 516 miles from Omaha.
This is a city, so called, and where many trains are made
up for the Black Hills.

Here is seen for the first time the Chinaman waiter, and
the beautiful " Lo" and the Chinaman are in close prox-
imity to each other here ; we are now over 6000 feet high,
and the Chinese are shoveling snow off the track for us
to pass through, and we are passing through snow sheds
again. Cheyenne is the capitol of Wyoming Territory,
and the county seat of Lorine County ; population some
6000 people. This is the place once known as hell on
wheels ; churches have come where godless people once
reigned. Judge Lynch once reigned here, and many a
gambler and bad man have been hung to the convenient
lamp post ; in fact the city authorities had their lamp
posts so arranged that a bad man could be strung up in
a jiffy ; and at one time Judge Lynch was so strict that
it was to be expected every morning to see one or more
of these gamblers and roughs hung up at any convenient
spot, but that kind of business was not suited to these
bad men, and they left for other parts more in accordance
with their sense of right and justice.

One word about the Black Hills. It is well known
that this country belongs to the Indians by reservation, but I think the whites have the best of it now,
and will keep it, provided the Government does not
interfere and drive out the white man. The Indian
is a dirty, nasty sneak, and a coward, and there is
no reason why he should have the best of our country and be fed by our Government in addition, and
I say, if the white man wants the Black Hills, let him
have them. The Indian never works on any of the reser-

vation lands given him ; his idea of living is to do nothing,
but creep around where the white man lives, and steal
from him enough to keep the breath of life in him ; then
go for the white man's scalp. Oh, it makes me shudder
when I think of the bad deeds of that beautiful " Lo !"
Painted from head to foot, as I have seen them so many
times, with a belt buckled around their waist, strung full
with weapons of warfare, the pistol, the tomahawk, the
scalping-knife. and the sharp-shooter, and many of them
with their bow and arrows strutting up and down the
railroad platforms, showing themselves to the white man,
and going through with their guttural jargon that no white
man can understand ; and when the train starts off many
of them jump on, strutting through the cars ; and they
never pay a cent for their rides. They are free to ride
just when and where they please, and no conductor dare
say a word to them ; while if a poor white man should
attempt to ride without paying he would be put off very
quick. You ask why are these devils allowed such privileges ? The answer is simple : The railroad officers are
afraid of them, and will do anything to appease the fan-
cied wrongs of the Indian. In other words, these redskins are the masters of the situation, and will remain so
until every redskin is sent to his happy hunting ground.
Yes, killed I say, for they are hated by all men, and the
sooner they are put out of sight as a class the better it
will be with the white man, but excuse me for expressing
my views so plainly on this subject.

Mountains are seen by this time, and they look pleasant, especially as we have been passing so long a time
over a level country. The first one of much account is
Hovney's Peak, 7,440 feet high. The Devil's Tower is one
of the most remarkable Peaks of the world—an immense
granite, 867 feet at its base, and 297 feet at the top, and
1,200 feet in height. Its summit is inaccessible to any
thing without wings. The Indian calls this shaft the
Bad God's place, from the fact that during thunder
storms the lightning plays around the top very beauti-

fully, which always frightens him, and he thinks that the Bad Spirit is angry with him, and that the Bad Spirit lives on the top of this peak.

We next come to Colorado, an empire of itself in enterprise, science, beauty, and the abundance of its pleasure resorts. I could write much about this beautiful place, but time will not permit, for I have much to tell you of places further on, and just as interesting. We now come to a place called Horace Greeley. This town was settled in May, 1870, by a small colony from the East. They purchased a tract of 100,000 acres of fine land in the valley of Lapowder River, the largest stream flowing eastward from the mountains of Colorado, and, curious to mention, this is a temperance town. No intoxicating drinks are sold here ; but this is of little consequence to those who will have it at any price, for the fire-water, as it is called out here, can be bought at the next town only six miles away ; but not selling it at all, has kept a class of loafers and idlers off who otherwise would have been a curse to any community.

We next come to a mountain, called the Mountain of the "Holy Cross," and, being the only one of the kind in the world, its fame is wide-spread.

Its height is 14,176 feet, and near the top is a cross made of two crevices running at right angles, and which are always filled with snow ; and the perpendicular arm of the cross is 1,500 feet long, while the horizontal arm of the cross is 700 feet long, and this cross can be seen for over 100 miles, the rocks on either side of the crevices forming it being of a very dark granite.

The next station is "Sherman," 549 miles from Omaha, and is noted for being the highest point on the railroad. We are now 8,242 feet above the level of the sea. The railroad here, at the time it was built, was higher than any other railroad in the world. The approach to this terrible elevation is so gradual that we hardly notice the ascent. It takes two powerful engines to pull up our long train ; and here we are—such a sight !—on the highest point on the continent of America. The air is so pure and light that a person feels, as if they had wings, they would go up higher. I got out of the cars and stepped on some rocks—procured a few specimens from a noted rock.

Near here are the graves of some men murdered by that beautiful animal called the Indian ; and these men are sleeping so near heaven.

A solitary pine tree is keeping sentinel over their graves. We have ascended in the last 32 miles over 2,200 feet, and now we begin to descend the other side of the Rocky Mountains, and it takes two engines to control the train, for, if one engine should fail to keep up steam, as it often happens on these long routes, the other is ready to do the work.

We now come to an iron-trussed bridge, called the Dale Creek Bridge—and it is one of the sights out West—it is 130 feet high and many feet long, and it is well worth a trip across the Continent to see this bridge. We now strike the great Laramer plains ; they average 40 miles wide and 100 miles long. They begin at the base of the Black Hills, and extend to the Medicine Bow mountains. They comprise an area of over 2½ million acres of the richest kind of grazing land, and many kind of cattle, sheep and horses, are seen feeding on them as we pass along.

The next object of interest is a Rock, called the Red Buttes, so called from the reddish color of the rocks. These rocks are of all kinds and shapes, many of them standing entirely alone, and then they are found in groups. The soil is of a reddish color also, and the geolists say it all indicates the presence of iron.

These Laramer plains have been called the paradise of sheep, and there are men here who own over 16,000 head, and these sheep are divided into droves of about 2,500 each. A man with a good pony and a shepherd dog can take care of a drove of that size without much trouble.

We have passed through to-day 14 long snow sheds, built in the rocky gorges of the rocky mountains.

This day, (April 13th), we are passing through a spur of the mountains, a grand sight indeed, and when I say a grand sight, I wish I could use the English language in such a way that you could just understand what I mean.

Right alongside of the track are mountains so high that you have almost to break your neck in bending back in order to look at their top, and such curious shaped rocks, many of them resembling castles that I have read of in story books, and of every conceivable shape and form.

We now come to a country where nothing grows much ; no grass, no trees, nothing but little tufts of Sage Brush, on the alkali plains and mountains. During the day we passed a number of coal shafts. Coal is being mined here in large quantities. At Laramie we got our breakfast, and a good one it was, at least we thought so ; and such appetites we had coming over the mountains and plains ; and they have a Soda mine at this place, and, in a little while, if properly developed, they can dig enough out of the ground to supply the whole world. In the neighborhood is a high rock, called the " Laramie Peak," the highest peak of the Black Hill range of mountains, and is 10,000 feet high.

Windmills are found in every hamlet and city. Deep wells are sunk in the plains, and the windmill pumps up the water for use. At every railroad station the windmill is seen ; probably no finer ones can be seen anywhere than on this railroad, and I will give you a description of a railroad windmill. They are 75 feet high, the base 25 feet across ; the tank for holding water is 37 feet high ; the arms of the windmill are 25 feet long, and the fan of the mill is 25 feet across. In the tank is a globe or ball floating in the water, and is so connected with levers that when the water has reached a certain height, the slats or fan are thrown in line with the wind, and the machine stops. As the water is drawn off the slats or fan are spread again, and the machine, operated upon by the wind, is again set in motion, and the pumping continues. Thus you see the whole thing is self-regulating and self-acting. The cost of mills of this pattern is $10,000.

Let me tell you how the noble red men bury their dead. The Comanches, Apaches, Cheyennes, Arapahoes and Kiowas, all bury their dead in some big tree. The manner of doing it is as follows : the corpse is securely wrapped up like a mummy. With it are placed food, arms, tobacco, etc., with which its spirit wants to go to the happy hunting grounds. Their feet are always turned towards the South. The whole pile is covered over with an outer covering made of willows, then the body is placed upon a platform, put in some large tree close at hand.

We now come to Black Buttes, and 'here the Railroad passes through deep cañons (or ravines) ; sometimes it seems, as you pass down the valley and look ahead, as though the train was going square against the rocks and would be dashed in pieces, but, a sudden curve, and you have rounded the projecting cliff and bluffs, and are safely passing on your journey ; again it seems as if the cliff and bluffs were trying to shake hands across the chasm or making an effort to become dovetailed toge-ther. They assume all kinds of shapes and forms, washed out in places by the storms of ages, smoothly carved as if by the hand of the sculptor, and again rug-ged and grotesque.

We next come to the Black Buttes, 795 miles from, Omaha, and 6,600 feet high. And we are now at Green River, where we get another good meal, and the land-lord keeps a sort of a museum that he has in cases in his ante-room—moss agates, fossil fish, petrified shells and petrified wood, and many others I have forgotten. I have with me three specimens of fossil fish in stone ; they are well worth studying. Many questions can be asked : How came these fish in stone so far up the mountain side ? is the first question. As I am not able to answer that, I will stop asking any more.

On Green River are many curiosities to look at—a high
projecting tower north of the track, a rock running up
625 feet like a shaft—a perpendicular rock at that—other
rocks in the neighborhood. The Twin Sisters will be
easily recognized by the traveler as he passes along.

Wake up ! Wake up ! exclaimed an old lady to her
sleeping husband, as they were passing this place, look
out and behold Solomon's Temple petrified. The sleepy
old man looked out and beheld what every traveler ex-
pects to see as they pass this wonderful collection of
rocks. One is called the Giant's Rock, and is a giant in
size, many feet high, and valuable for the many formations of curious plants and fishes contained in it. At the
top, or near the top, are found formations of plants,
while near the base, say 100 feet further down, you will
find the remains of fishes, all belonging to the fresh
water kind, and all of them extinct.

With the fishes are found specimens of birds' feathers
and a few reeds. Another rock, near by, is called the
Giant's Tea Kettle, and a very nice natural shape it is
too, with the spout of the kettle sticking out.

We next come to Rock Springs, where a great number
of Chinamen are living. From this out we shall come
across this kind of help at all the hotels, and doing the
work that our servants are doing at home. They are a
curious kind of people, and must be studied to be understood. They are renowned for their industry and econo-
my ; they will comfortably live upon what our people
throw away.

We now come to "Echo Cañon," with full breath,
anxious heart and keen zest. We scan the scenes from
the car window or platform, and prepare for one grand,
rushing descent, into the glorious Echo Cañon. I will
never forget the feeling of wonder and awe we experienced while riding through this wonderful Cañon.—
Scenes, beside which all those of the East are pigmies in
comparison, astoundingly abrupt and massive ; and the
little company of spectators seemed but an insignificant

portion of the handiwork of the Almighty. The train which we were on seemed only as baby carriages, and the shriek of the whistle, as it echoed and resounded from rock to rock, appeared to me like entering the portals of the palace of some terrible being. But, Brothers, the thoughts of the things seen in the space of less than three hours, even now, overpowers me.

You must remember, however, that the scenes witnessed from the railroad are but a very little portion of the whole. To gather true, refreshing glimpses of Western scenery, the tourist must get away from the railroad into the little valleys, ascend the bluffs and mountains, and views, yet more glorious, will greet the eye. Echo Cañon is the most impressive scene that is beheld for over 1,500 miles on the overland railroad. The constant succession of rocks—each growing more and more huge, and more and more perpendicular and colossal in form— make the attractions of the valley *grow upon the eye*, instead of decrease.

We enter the cañon about on a level with the top of the rocks, and in our case overlook them, then gradually descend, until at the very bottom of the valley the track is so close to the foot of the rocks that we have to elevate our heads with an upward look, not less than 90°, to scale their summits. Let us now prepare to descend, and brace ourselves eagerly for the exhilaration of the ride, the scenery of which will live with us in memory for years to come—and, as we pass down this deep gorge, you will want to look with all the eyes you have, and look quick too, as one object passes quickly out of sight as another comes into view.

We come at last to Castle Rock Station, right in the Echo Cañon ; and it is called from a rock very near, looking very much like a castle. Notice the arch doorway on one corner of the old castle, with red-colored side pieces, capped with grey. Near by are some needle rocks, sharp-pointed, one small one especially prominent. Opposite the water tanks are rocks, worn in curious shapes. Next come the rock called the Swallow's Nest, so called from the great number of holes near the top, chiselled out by the action of water and wind, and in summer a large number of swallows make this place their home.

Then comes a honeycombed peak, with a shelving gray rock under it ; then comes a singular perpendicular column, jutting out in front of the ledge with outstretched wings, as if it would lift itself up and fly, but for its weight; and this is called Eagle Rock. If there was a projection in front to resemble the neck and head, the rock would appear very much like an eagle, with pinions extended just ready to fly. Then comes the Hanging Rocks, then the—but I cannot tell you any more about these rocks, for the subject is too great to attempt to make it any plainer. But we now come to some rocks and stones piled up by Brigham Young in 1857 to roll down on General Albert Sidney Johnson's army, when it should pass here for Salt Lake City. The cañon verily becomes a gorge here, and the wagon-road runs close to the base of the high bluffs, which the Mormons fortified after a fashion. High up you see these piles of stones. They look very small, but nevertheless they are there for the very purpose just mentioned. At the time spoken of there was trouble with the Mormons at Salt Lake City, which is but a short distance from here, and troops were sent to quell the disturbance ; and Brigham Young knowing that the troops would have to pass through this gorge, sent men there to stop them by hurling upon them the stones from this lofty place. The question is asked, did they roll down these stones ? They did not, because it was late in the season, and before the army came to this place it went into winter quarters this side, and when Spring came, the disturbance was settled and the army was called back, but the stones are there yet for any one to examine for himself. We next come to a rock projecting out, called the Steamboat Rock, very much resembling that vessel, and the stone is of a reddish cast—a little cedar, like a flag of perpetual green, shows its head on the bow. Further on is another rock, projecting out, very plain, and resembles the vessel called the "Great Republic;" they are really curious formations. And still another rock—nearly resembles the Great Eastern—and all these rocks are really very curious shaped, and wonderful to those who see them for the first time.

Sentinel Rock comes next, and it is within a cove, and seems withdrawn from the rest in front, and many more curious rocks can be seen if the train would only stop and give us a chance to examine these wonderful structures; but as it will not, the next thing is to get as good a look as possible.

And now we pass into "Weber Cañon," which almost equals its sister the Echo Cañon.

The first rock of prominence is the Pulpit Rock, standing out clear and distinct from all other rocks in the neighborhood. It is said that Brigham Young preached from this pulpit on his way to Salt Lake City. This rock is 60 feet above the track; all these rocks just spoken of are over 800 feet above the Railroad track.

We next come to a station called "Echo," a beautiful place nestling among the mountains, with evidences of thrift on every hand; and the place is rightly named, for any kind of a loud noise is echoed from every side, and the reverberation of a cannon shot is actually astounding.

The rocks of Weber Cañon are even more singular than those of the Echo Cañon. After leaving Echo we soon notice on the north side of the track two curious formations. The first is a group of reddish-colored cones, of different sizes, and varying some in shape, but, on the whole, remarkably uniform in their appearance. These are known as the Battlement Rocks. Next comes the weird forms of "The Witches," looking as though they were talking to each other, of a gray color. How these columns were ever formed is a question of interest to the geologist. One of these Witches, at least, looks as if she was afflicted with the Grecian Bend; and all of these rocks stand as if they were mocking time and its changes. High up on the face of a bluff, to the left as you pass through the gorge, you will see little holes or caves worn by the elements. In these holes the eagles build their nests. This bluff is called "Eagle Nest Rock." Every year the proud monarch of the air finds here a safe place for her young. It is beyond the reach of man, and accessible only to the birds of the air.

We now pass from these wonderful structures of red and yellow stone to one of peace and quietness, for we come out into a broad and spacious plain, called the Great Salt Lake Plains, dotted here and there with numerous houses, and, what to us is very peculiar, we noticed that the houses here had many doors of entrance on either side. On inquiring, we are told that these houses belong to Mormons, and each apartment on the first floor contains a family of one wife and her children, and of course, they never intrude on their neighbors' premises, but have a door to come in and go out of their own ; and so it is now understood among us, when we see a house with more than one door for entrance, we count the doors to tell how many wives there are inside.

We next come to a Tree, which is looked for by the passengers, as we are told such a tree does exists, and on this tree hangs a sign with these words, "1,000 Miles from Omaha," and it is the only tree for some distance from this place.

High up on the rocks, to the right as you pass ahead, see how the storms have made holes in projecting points, through which light and sky beyond can be observed. Now look back and see another similar formation on the opposite side—one to be seen looking ahead, the other looking back.

I should have mentioned, when giving the description about the rocks, and told you of another rock, called the Devil's Slide. This Slide is represented by two tiers of granite stone, about 14 feet apart, standing on their edges, running from the top of the mountain to its base ;

and I said about 14 feet apart, wide enough to let the
devil slide in without hitting either side. There is a
smooth surface between these two ledges, and they are
about 800 feet long, up and down the mountain. The
devil, I am told, takes this method to get down the mountain, by sliding down the inclined plane, when he is in a
hurry to catch some Eastern train coming around the
bend. At the bottom of the slide is quite a body of water
for the devil to slake his thirst when calling on his friends
aboard the trains from the East, as the devil never drinks
anything stronger than water, although whisky was first
made by him—he leaves that for man to drink.

We have now passed through the Wahsatch Mountains, and have come into what I have mentioned before,
a beautiful plain, with all the beauties of farms and farm
houses, the lands reclaimed from the waste of a dreary
desert and made to blossom as the rose; for, as before
mentioned, we are now in the Great Salt Lake Valley,
and we have at last arrived at Ogden, the terminus of the
U. P. R. R. Co. in the West; and here we leave the
main road for Salt Lake City, which is about 37 miles
from here, going in a southerly direction.

But before arriving in the Great Salt Lake Basin,
you pass through the Devil's Gap with the Devil's Gate,
and several other odd characteristics about it. It is
one of the most remarkable places on the line of the road.
The waters of the Weber River, as if enraged at their attempted restraint, rush wildly along—now on one side
of the road and now on the other; and now, headed off
completely by a projecting ledge before them, turn madly
to the right, determined, with irresistible strength, to
force their way through the mountain. Foiled in this,
they turn abruptly to the left, still rushing madly on,
and at last find their way out to the plains beyond. If
Echo was grand and Weber grander, the Devil's Gate is
the grandest of them all.

We arrived at Ogden at 5 P. M , and two hours later
started for the Mormon settlement, and arrived there at 9

o'clock, P. M., and went to the Walker House, kept by a gentile.

The next morning I started out to hunt up an Odd Fellow. I was directed to a very large man on the other side of the street ; I introduced myself, and learned he was the Noble Grand of one of the Lodges in the city. I had a very pleasant time with him, and while in conversation asked him how polygamy was looked upon by the Odd Fellows. He answered very promptly by saying that Odd Fellowship had nothing to do with Brigham Young or his opinions ; that they did not mix with men who had more than one wife, and would black-ball every one who was proposed of the Mormon faith.

As he spoke so positive, I thought I would ask him about Odd Fellowship and Catholicism. His answer was the same. I left him and went on my voyage of discovery. But, Brothers, that great big man told me a lie— an awful lie—when he was giving the Mormons such a running down and talking about black-balling them, for at that moment he was a Mormon himself, with five wives ; he afterwards told Past-Grand Master Barnes how he stuffed me, and in open Lodge, in San Francisco, Bro. Barnes told the whole story, and I was there and heard him. Well, after leaving this beautiful "liar," I took a carriage, with my family, and rode about to see the Mormon sights.

I learn that old Brigham is not at home, but attending a conference of his Saints 300 miles south, at St. George, and dedicating a Mormon temple. He is 76 years old, is quite feeble, and, as he cannot walk much, he has a three-wheeled carriage made to hurdle himself around in.

We observed the people quite sharp to-day, and have come to the conclusion that the Mormons look and act as other people do. Business is here conducted on the same plan as in other cities. The population is about 25,000, and trading is conducted as elsewhere ; in fact, everything passes off in an orderly way. We visited, of course, the Mormon temple, but let me tell you first about the head devil of polygamy.

Born in Vermont, June 1st, 1801, he is 76 years old. He joined the Mormons in 1833, at Kirtland, Ohio. At the death of Joseph Smith, the original Mormon, he was elected President and Prophet of the Mormon faith. In 1846 he announced that Salt Lake Valley had been revealed to him as the promised land, and founded Salt Lake City in July, 1847. In 1849 the Mormons had so increased that they formed a State, and called it the Desert, but Congress refused to admit such a State into the Union by that name, but, in 1850, Brigham Young was appointed Governor of the Territory, and continued so until 1854 ; but the Mormons got ugly and defied the laws of the United States, and Buchanan, in 1857, appointed Alfred Cummings, Governor, and sent an army of 2,500 men to uphold his authority.

In 1857 the Governor declared the Mormon Territory in a state of rebellion, but, in 1858, the next year, a compromise was effected by which the proper authority was to be respected, and old Brigham was left in power, as Governor, again. He is six feet tall, and uncommonly compact and muscular. He measures 44 inches around the waist ; his head is of moderate size ; his hair is chestnut in color, abundant in growth, and combed in a style to the right side of the head, hanging like the cap of a rooster's comb. He has nineteen wives ; 15 of them are his for time and eternity, the other four are wives by proxy, widows of Joseph Smith, the original Mormon. The children of the four wives, by Brigham, are credited to Joseph Smith, numbering say 15, and go to swell Joseph Smith's kingdom.

All Brigham's wives are called by their maiden names, to distinguish them one from the other. The following is a correct list of Brigham's wives, in the order of their marriage : Mary Ann Angle. Lucy Decker, Mrs. Augusta Erble, Harriet Cook, Clara Decker (sister to Lucy), Emeline Free, Lucy Bigelow, Zina D. Huntington, Susan Snively, Margaretta Pierce, Mrs. Freiss, Emily Partridge, Martha Boker, Eliza Burgess, Eliza R. Snow,

Harriet Borney, Amelia Folsom—his favorite, called Princess Amelia—Mary Van Cott, and Ann Eliza Webb, the nineteenth and last. This very much married man has only 45 children living ; the most of them are grown up and married—29 girls and 16 boys. Seven of Brigham's daughters taste the sweets of plural marriage; two of the seven call Hiram B. Cleason husband ; two call George Thucker husband, and two are married to Mark Croxwell ; the seventh is the second mate of Thomas Williams.

Amelia Folsom, called Princess Amelia, is the only one old Brigham lives with, he has forsaken all the others, and upon the Princess he bestows his kindness, care and attention. In his household they have what they call ration days ; once a month each family receives 5 lbs. sugar, 1 lb. candles, a bar of soap and a box of matches. The rule with all of them (except the Princess) is that all food, except the plainest, and all clothing, except what nature requires, the wife must procure for herself and children. Brigham promised to give them $1,000 each a year for pin money, and a good home, but they get nothing from him, and they are obliged to earn their own and their children's living.

These Mormons have certain ceremonies and oaths when they take persons into their fold, but they amount to nothing, except when they take a solemn oath to bear eternal hostility to the government of the United States, and avenge the murder of their Prophet, Joseph Smith. In this ceremony the women have a long robe, which is placed on the right shoulder, is gathered at the waist, and falls to the floor.

The men wear a cap of linen, similar to those worn by stone-masons, and this is the costume in which a Mormon is buried. We all went through Princess Amelia's house, a new one, building for her by Brigham. It is a very pretty building, four stories high, standing on a high point of the Prophet's grounds. When on the roof we could look far away for many miles, and a beautiful sight it was.

The next thing to tell you is about the city itself. First, the discovery. Brigham landed here in 1847, 30 years ago. At that time it was a dreary waste, but yet a beautiful site, so far as location is concerned, for a city. This city lies on a gradual slope from the Wahsatch mountains, which tower up behind it on the east to River Jordan on the west. Orson Pratt, one of Brigham's faithful ones, was sent to spy out the land. He did this, and on the 22d day of July, 1847, he rode over the valley, then returned to the main body, and reported to Brigham, when the whole encampment went to view the land themselves. On the 24th of July they arrived on the top of the hill, overlooking the site of the city and the valley beyond. They were enchanted with the scene, and gave vent to their joy in exclamations of praise to God; finally, believing that they had found the land of promise, though it did not flow with milk and honey, the Zion of the mountains, predicted by the ancient prophets. The Mormons are great in literal interpretations—to them the Bible means just what it says. They had reasons, however, for rejoicing. The Great Salt Lake glittered like silver in the rays of the sun, before them, the towering mountains, crowned with clouds and snow, lifted themselves up toward the sky, and the valley, though a desert, was as lovely as a June rose.

The party encamped on a stream, and proceeded to consecrate the whole valley to the Kingdom of God.— Four days after, the ground for the Temple was selected, consisting of 40 acres, and a city two miles square was laid out, streets 40 rods wide were staked off, and the blocks contained 10 acres each.

Orson Pratt took the observations, and determined the latitude and longitude of the place. A large number of this pioneer party, after planting their crops, returned for their families. The last party for that year arrived on the last day of October, and they were received with great rejoicing.

Brigham went back with the returning party, and did

not return to Zion again until the following year. After
that immigration from foreign countries came flooding
in in masses ; the city grew, and the people spread out
over the territory, settling every available spot of land,
and this contributed to the prosperity of the country.

Now, I have been thus particular in describing this
place to you, as I suppose it is not generally known how
the Mormons first started this City of Zion, the Mecca to
which all good Mormons look, and expect to see before
they are called to visit brother Joseph in the other world.

In looking around, the first thing to see is the Sulphur
Springs, for a bath ; and these are, to invalids, the most
splendid and delightful places of resort in the city—exceedingly valuable for rheumatism or dyspepsia, and
they are excellent in invigorating properties, and especially good in skin diseases.

The Sulphur Springs are about one mile from our
hotel, and can be reached either by horse-car or carriage.
The best time to enjoy them is early in the morning, before breakfast, or just before dinner—never to be taken
within three hours after eating. These springs issue from
the limestone rocks near the base of the mountain. You
· can get here the Turkish hot-air and the Russian bath in
addition to the natural bath.

From the sulphur bath we went a mile further on, and
came to the Hot Springs ; and here we found hot water,
boiling right out of the mountain side, issuing from limestone rocks, and it boils up with great force ; the temperature is near 200 degrees. Meat can be boiled for the
table in a few minutes, and eggs can be boiled in three
minutes.

The next place to visit is the Museum. This was not
much of a sight for us, and so we went to the grand
pavillion, called the Tabernacle, a building that will seat
13,000 inside, and there is not a pillar or column to inter
cept the sight. The building inside is 250 feet × 150 feet.
To upold the roof, there is built outside of the church,
and, next to it, 46 pillars, 9 feet deep and 3 feet wide—

these form the base for the rafters of the roof to rest upon, which are a strong lattice-work of timbers firmly bolted together and self-supporting. The ceiling is 62 feet high, and perforated with holes for ventilation.

The west end is occupied with a platform on which rests a very large organ. This organ was built in the church by the Mormons themselves. The singers sit here, also from this platform Brigham dispenses the Gospel to his congregation. The bishops of this church sit here, also, in twelve rows. In the centre of the church is a large fountain of water, walled up with small granite stones. I walked up to the fountain, took one of the stones and brought it home as a gift from the temple.— The Mormon who was with me, showing the temple, said nothing, and so one of the stones from the temple is in the house of a gentile for exhibition here.

Brigham Young's grounds are surrounded with a very high fence, made of mud and stone cemented together. This fence is not easily scaled, and inside his grounds are laid out as only money, tact, and wit, can direct ; gentiles are not generally admitted to these grounds.

On these grounds is the Endowment House, of which so much has been said and written. In this building all the marriages are performed and other rites of the church are conducted. No gentile's eye is ever permitted to look upon the altar where polygamy is so successfully carried on.

Nearly opposite to this building is a large and beautiful house that belongs to Princess Amelia, called the Amelia Palace, and it is one of the places shown to visitors. There were many other objects of interest, which time will not permit me to mention ; but I want to call your attention to the manner of irrigation conducted in this city. This city was originally laid out in ten acre lots, running at right angles. Now there is a large stream of water flowing from the mountains back of the city, and this stream is made to run along the upper edge of the city, and from this large stream many smaller streams

flow into the streets, running down the hill or descent of
the city, for this city is partially built on a side hill, con-
sequently each street has a stream, greater or smaller, as
the water may be used, and at the corner of each street
is built a kind of wooden lock to turn the water one way
or the other. The city is divided into wards, and each
ward has its master, and he compels all of the inhabi-
tants to turn out and work on public improvements.—
There is no shirking—every one has a responsibility to
guard and watch his own property and take care of his
irrigating ditches and keep his ward in perfect order.
This city is in perfect order and quietness, more so than
any other city I was ever in, and so, go where you will,
you will find running water, and plenty of it, too, so that
it carries off all impurities, and to-day Salt Lake City is
the most healthy of any on this Continent. Now, I have
just one other place to mention before leaving Salt Lake
City, and that is the Great Salt Lake itself. This lake is
about 20 miles from the city ; so one morning my son
Frank and myself got up very early and took a narrow-
guaged railroad that runs across the head of the lake
into the mines in the mountains.

We stopped at a place called Lake Point, and we went
down to the water. We found a good dock and bathing
houses, also, a large steamboat for summer excursions,
with a stern wheel, called a Mississippi Steamboat. We
found the captain and his wife on board, and they treated
us very kindly.

I drew up some of the water and tasted it, and found
it very salt indeed. The lady gave me a small bottle of
salt that she had gathered last summer off the shores of
the lake. The salt will crystalize, and a crust of salt
will be formed on shore almost any fine day. No fish of
any kind will live in this lake, neither will a person
swimming sink in it, the only thing you have to do is to
keep your head up and not get your feet where your
head ought to be. A person can walk from the shore
into the water up to his arm-pits, and then he will float.

This lake is about 100 miles long by 50 miles wide. The water looks very blue.

We walked about the shore and picked up quite a quantity of curious stones, thrown up by the waves ; we had our dinner at the hotel near by, and then took the train for the city. While at Salt Lake City I attended a gentile mass meeting. It was gotten up against Mormonism. The outsiders, or Gentiles, as they are called here, are in arms against the Mormons ; I tell you, the gentiles gave old Brigham fits ; they talk very bitter against him, and are determined to break up Mormonism, root and branch, in this city, but my opinion is they have a big job on hand—however, the Gentiles are getting in the majority, and they talk plainer now than they did some years ago.

Sunday, April 15th, was a very still day, and we spent it very quietly as pleasure-seekers. No rum-shops were open. The people here go to church, both old and young—they drop all kinds of business and attend church ; the Sabbath schools are well attended, also.

With other guests of our hotel, I went to a Mormon church in the 18th ward. There is no service held in the Tabernacle during the winter months, because the building is so large they have no way of warming it ; but each ward has a Mormon chapel, and services are held in them on Sunday. In the one that I attended the services were much after the form of the Campbellites in Illinois, years ago. They have preaching by one of the elders, and it is difficult to distinguish much difference between them and the Methodists of our own city. At all their meetings they have bread and water administered before parting. The preaching was Christ, and him crucified, and called on all classes to repent of their sins and come to Christ to be saved ; but the cursed sin of polygamy kills off all the good they may do, in my estimation.

On Saturday night I visited an Odd Fellow's Lodge, called Jordan Lodge, No. 3. I was received in due

form, and invited to take a seat to the right of the Noble
Grand. I found they were better posted in the unwritten
work than I had expected. The Grand Master of Utah
Territory, L. P. Higbee, was there, and other distinguished
brothers also. The Grand Master exemplified the unwritten work, and did it well, too, hardly missing a
word, the same as P. G. M. Stebbins, when here, a
year ago.

This Jordan Lodge had preferred charges against one
of its members, for conduct unbecoming an Odd Fellow.
The Lodge members upheld the erring brother, but the
Grand officers being in attendance, they heard the testi-
mony, and when the Grand Lodge of that Territory met,
at Ogden, the following week, they passed a resolution
requesting Jordan Lodge to expel the erring brother, and
if they would not, or could not, then the Grand Lodge
would expel the Lodge from all the privileges of our
order. I have never heard just how the Lodge settled
the case ; Jordan Lodge did not close till midnight.

Tuesday morning, April 17th, in company with the
Grand officers, I took the train for Ogden, to attend the
Grand Lodge of the Territory of Utah. We arrived in
due time, and there I found P. G. M. Barnes, of the
Heart and Hand, also P. G. Alexander, ·of New York
City ; I tell you I was glad to see them.

The Grand Lodge of the Territory of Utah convened,
and I was introduced to the Grand Lodge by D. G. M.
Hemingdray, in a neat speech. The Grand Master responded at length, and received me in the name of the
Grand Lodge of Utah. I took my seat among the brothers, and in a few minutes it appeared to me as if I was
at home among my own brothers, for they did their best
to make me feel so. I remained with the brothers until
5 P. M., then took leave of them, shaking hands with
every man, from the Grand Master to the Outside Guar-
dian, in the ante-room, and then strolled down to the
Depot to meet my folks from Salt Lake City. They were
on hand in time, and at 7 o'clock, P. M., we were in our
drawing-room ready to continue our journey westward.

LECTURE NO. 3.

BROTHERS : My second lecture left us at Ogden, in a palace drawing-room car, at 7 P. M., April 17th, 1877, ready to start westward again.

The first thing of notice are the steaming hot springs close on the right of the track. These springs are of both iron and sulphur, and from the sediment deposited over quite an area of ground near by, I should think that iron predominated.

The first town of note we come to is Corinne, 857 miles from San Francisco. Here is an Odd Fellow's Lodge : though the brothers are not many in number, yet they are very zealous in the good work ; and here Mormonism has no hold in the city.

On the completion of the R. R. here, the gentiles took possession of the town, and they were determined to maintain their ascendency. From that time, this place has been an object of defamation by the Mormons.

In early history this town was a rough place ; but the roughs have passed on, or they fill unknown graves, and the town is governed by men of character and religious principles.

We soon arrive at Promontory Point, 804 miles from San Francisco. It is here where the two roads meet, the U. P. R. R. from the East, and the C. P. R. R. from the West. On the 10th day of May, 1869, the marriage took place.

If I had the time I would like to tell you just how this whole thing was done, but it would take too long ; yet I will give you some of the facts. At 8 A. M. spectators began to arrive ; at 9 A. M. the whistle of the C. R. from the west was heard, bringing a large number of dignita-

.ries to witness this, the grandest scene ever performed by man. Just before noon the announcement was made at Washington that the driving of the last spike of the R. R. was then going on, and thus the great R. R. would be a positive fact; and instantly, at Washington, a great crowd gathered around the telegraph office to hear the final report.

The manager of the telegraph company placed a magnetic ball where all present could see it, and connected the same with the main line, notifying the places all along the lines of telegraph that he was ready, and instantly New York, San Francisco and Boston announced that they were ready. In San Francisco the lines were connected with the alarm bell in the tower, where the heavy ringing of the bell might speed the news immediately over the city as quick as the event was completed. Waiting for some time in impatience, at last came this message from Promontory Point: "Almost ready—hats off, prayer is being offered." A silence for the prayer ensued. The bell tolled again, and the office at Promontory Point said: "We have got done praying, and the spike is about to be presented." Chicago replied: "We understand all are ready in the East." Answer came: "All are ready—now the spike will soon be driven—the sign will be three dots from the commencement of the blows." For a moment all was silent, and then the hammer of the magnet tapped the bell, 1, 2, 3, the signal. Another pause of a few moments, and the lightning came flashing back "Done," and the great American Continent was successfully spanned. Immediately thereafter there flashed over the lines the announcement to the Associated Press these words: "The last rail is laid, the last spike is driven, the Pacific R. R. is completed;" and the point of junction is 1,086 miles west from Missouri River and 690 miles east from Sacramento.

Such were the telegraphic incidents that attended the completion of the greatest work of the age ; but, during these few expectant moments, the scene itself, at Pro-. montory Point, was very impressive.

After the rival engines had made up toward each other, a call was made for the masses to stand back, so that all could see. Prayer was offered by the Rev. Dr. Todd, of Massachusetts, remarks were made by General Doyle and Gov. Sanford, three cheers were given for the Government of the U. S., for the R. R., for the President, for the Star Spangled Banner, for the owners, and for those who furnished the means. Four spikes were then presented—two of them were gold, and the other two were silver.

They were furnished by Montana, Idaho, California and Nevada.. They were each about seven inches long, and a little larger than the ordinary railroad spike.

Dr. Harkness, of Sacramento, delivered Gov. Sanford a spike of pure gold, and a speech attending it; Hon. F. A. Frittle, of Nevada, presented a spike of pure silver, with this beautiful remark : " To the Iron of the East, and the Gold of the West, Nevada adds the link of Silver to span the Continent and weld the Oceans together." Dr. Durand stood on the north side of the rail and Gov. Sanford on the south side. At a given signal these two gentlemen struck the spikes, and at the same time the electric spark was sent through the wires in all directions, giving the joyful tidings ; then the engines moved up a little nearer, until they touched each other, and a bottle of wine was poured on the rail as a libation. Immediately after these ceremonies were finished, the rail, the ties and nails were removed for safe keeping, and in their place ordinary ones were substituted.

Now, Brothers, I have been much longer telling you just how this wonderful work was finished than I first intended; but if you are satisfied, I am, and so we will pass on our journey.

We next come to a station called the " Lake," and here I find a board sticking up alongside of the track, saying that just here the constructing employees laid ten miles of railroad in one day—a pretty good day's

work, you may say—yes, that is so ; but you must recollect that we are still passing over the plains, very
level country, alkali though it be, and they had over
6,000 Chinamen to work on the road.

The next point of attention is a place called Monument,
804 miles from 'Frisco. An isolated rock rises like a monument in the lake on the left, while the hill on the right
is crowned with turrets and projecting rocks and domes.

We next come to Lucin, a station 734 miles from
San Francisco. Just beyond here we strike Grouse
Creek, which rises in the hills north. This creek sinks
in the Sandy Desert, for we are now on the Great American Sandy Desert, and this is the first water that we
come to that sinks into the earth, and has no outlet as
other streams have.

As we near the next station, called "Tecoma," the
traveler will notice a small granite monument on the left
side of the track, marking the Nevada State. As we pass
this monument, we enter the land of the Big Bonanza.

Tecoma, the station that we are at now, is celebrated
for being the station of the Tecoma mines, owned by
Howland & Aspinwall, of New York City.

Leaving Tecoma, the railroad continues over a sage
brush and grease wood plains ; and, as we travel over
these plains, we approach the grand old Pilot Peak, the
landmark for many miles on this road, and is held in
great regard by the emigrant trains crossing the plains of
the dreary Desert. We must keep in mind also, that we
are, at this place, near 6,000 feet high.

The next is Dead Man's Spring Station. A man was
found dead here one morning, killed by his partner, who
fled with all of the dead man's traps. The news spread,
the man was chased into another State, convicted, and
sentenced to be hung. The mob collected, took him
from the jail ; the next morning he was found hanging
to a telegraph pole, and the spring is called the Dead
Man's Spring to this day.

We are now passing into the far-famed Humboldt Valley, 669 miles from San Francisco ; Humboldt Wells are next passed—there are about thirty of them. As no volcanic evidences appear here, these wells must be natural ones, and from the nature of the soil about here, these wells do not rise and pass away, as other wells do, in a more compact soil. This is the great watering station for all kinds of trains, trails, emigrant stations, and so forth. The Grass Creek, the Thousand Spring Valley, and the Cedar Pass Roads, all meet at this place. Emigrants always rejoice when they have passed the perils of the Great American Desert and arrived at these springs, where there is plenty of water and abundance of grass for their weary and worn animals ; hence it is a favorite camping ground.

We are now at Elcho Station, celebrated as a watering station. North, one mile from here, are six wells or springs, three of hot water and three of cold. The hot springs show 185° Fahrenheit, and one of them is called the Chicken Soup Spring. With a little salt and pepper for seasoning, the water tastes very much like chicken broth.

We will now take our leave of this city, and refreshed with food and rest, we resume our westward trip. The valley continues to widen for a few miles as we advance, and in the cool morning, clouds of steam can be seen rising from the hot springs on the left.

We soon cross Susan's Creek, then Maggie's Creek, then Amelia's Creek, then Mary's Creek, and this brings us up to "Carlin," 585 miles from San Francisco, and 5,000 feet high. In the vicinity of Carlin, the four little creeks come in from the north, in the order in which they are named—"Susie," "Maggie," "Amelia," and "Mary." These four creeks are named after an emigrant family, who passed through here in the early days of traveling to the Far West, and, as the father of this family saw these four creeks, he named them as above-mentioned, to perpetuate the memory of his family of four girls.

Next in order is Shoshone, an Indian village so called. Fenimore Cooper would doubtless call it an Indian village, but it requires a great stretch of imagination on the part of an American, or a live Yankee, to see it in that light. A dozen or so of tents, discolored with smoke and besmeared with dirt and grease, revealing from six to ten squalid beings, covered with vermin, filth, and rags, is not calculated to create a pleasing impression, or waken imaginary flights to any great extent.

These Indians are called the Shoshones ; their reservation proper is at Carlin, but for some reason best known to themselves they are never found there, but prefer looking out for themselves, by stealing from the travelers rather than to be taken care of by the agency for Indians. These Indians are inveterate gamblers, and a group of squaws will sit for many hours on the ground around a blanket, stretched out, and throw sticks. There are usually five of these sticks, from four to five inches long, and painted on one side. Each squaw has a rock, or a piece of coal, or some other hard substance along side of her. She will gather these sticks, and give them a toss up, so that they will fall on the hard substance, and will bound from that to the blanket, and the point of the game is to see how many of these painted sides shall come upon the blanket. It seems to be a per- fect game of chance, and the one who can turn up the most painted sides has the game.

We again come to Hot Springs, near the Maiden's Grave; this stream comes from the mountain side. The water is boiling hot, and partakes of sulphur.

We are coming into the cattle region again. On the other side of the Rocky Mountains a man by the name of Iliff took the lead in cattle; but here are men who can sell him and his cattle, and then have as many head of cattle to spare as he had at first.

The Humboldt Valley and its tributaries constitute the best part of the State for stock ranges; the snow does not fall very deep, does not stop very long, and the grass makes its appearance very early in the Spring.

We are now at Battle Mountain, 524 miles from San Francisco, located at the junction of Rese River and Humboldt Valley. This is the regular dinner station, and the passengers dine at a cosy and attractive place, and here the traveler will listen to the beautiful "Ah Sin." This town is in a lumber country ; here also a battle was fought with the red skins, who had a hankering after the stock of the white man, but "Lo" got the worst of it, as the story runs.

Hot springs are found here also, nearly sixty of them, covering nearly half a section of land. The largest is about sixty feet long, by thirty feet wide, and at times rises and falls from three to five feet.

Leaving Battle Mountain, we have a straight track for about twenty miles across a sage-brush plain, the Humboldt River being on our right.

Stone House soon comes to view, 504 miles from San Francisco; quite a number of battles have been fought here between the whites and the Indians, and many graves can be seen on both sides of the track as we pass along. Hot springs are seen here also; in fact, hot springs are found at almost every station from this out, and seem to denote that this is nothing but a volcanic country.

We are now at Winimucca, 463 miles from San Francisco. It was named in honor of a chief of that name of the Piute Indians—the name itself means chief. This town is the county seat of Humboldt County. The Piutes have their tents scattered in all directions here, to which the name of Wick-ee-up is given. They seem to remind one of departed glory, if they ever had any— the Indian race I mean. I have not much to say in honor of an Indian, but of *this* tribe, to their honor be it said, licentiousness among their women is very rare, and virtue is held in high esteem; but very few half-breeds can be found, or are known in the State. This tribe, with the Bannocks, were especially hostile to the whites in early days, and fought for many years with desperation and cruelty to prevent the settlement and development of this country. This courage and deadly enmity has been displayed on many a hard-fought field; and if there are families in the East or on the Pacific who still mourn the loss of missing ones, who were last heard from as crossing the plains, some Indian warrior yet living might be able to explain the mystery which has enveloped their final fate.

For a number of years they hung around the trains of emigrants with ceaseless vigilance, eager to dispatch a stray victim, and upon the borders of settlements, ready to strike down the hardy pioneer at the first favorable opportunity; but at present, overpowered by numbers, they live upon the bounty of their former enemies, and are slowly learning the ways of civilization. As a class, they are still indolent, dirty, and covered with vermin ; but they begin to learn the worth of money, and know already that it has a purchasing power which will supply their scanty wardrobe and satisfy their longing appetites.

In passing down this plain we see, on our left, a mountain, said to be the highest peak in this country, 8,000 feet high. It is called Star Peak, and its lofty summit is always covered with snow. Opposite this mountain is Humboldt, 423 miles from San Francisco.

We now arrive at an oasis in the desert. The traveler from the East will be especially delighted with Humboldt ; it will remind him of things human, and of living in a land of cultivation again. The first growing tree since leaving Ogden will here be seen, with green grass and flowing fountains. Humboldt House is a regular breakfast and supper station, at which passengers stop for meals. A fountain, surrounded with an iron fence, springs up in front of the house, while gold fish swim around in the basin below. East of the house, locust and poplar trees are growing finely, while the ground is covered thickly with blue grass. Alkali grass was first grown, and was very profitable, and a plot of this grass has been cut from five to seven times in one season. This is a pretty tough story, but yet it is a fact.

The average growth of potatoes is 300 bushels to the acre, and of the very best quality.

Here, almost in the midst of the Great Nevada Desert, with barenness and desolation on every hand, with a high, rocky mountain on one side, and a huge alkali flat on the other, nestled under the towering cliffs as though it would claim shelter and protection, is this *oasis* in the desert, this reminder of more genial climes and a more kindly soil. This relief from the wearisome, dreary views which have everywhere met our gaze over the largest part of our journey, and the experiment so successfully accomplished here, prove, beyond a doubt, that the desert can be redeemed and made to blossom as the rose ; grit, labor, and above all, water, will do it.

This place and its surroundings cause the traveler not only to rejoice over the scene which here greets his gaze, but serves to remind him of his home—of God's country, either in the far east, or at this point, in the nearer west.

Many mines of sulphur are found in the mountains near here, and they furnish employment for a great many men. These mines are covered with ashes ; in fact, wherever these mines are found, there you will find the white ashes, indicating that at some period they were on fire, and that the fire was smothered by the accumulation of ashes. When the elements shall melt with a fervent heat, the vast sulphur deposits of Nevada will add fuel to the flames, and greatly accelerate the melting process.

As we leave Humboldt, we immediately come into Alkali Plains, or Desert, as it is called here, covering a very large area of ground. Of all the dreary wastes to be seen in this section of country, this desert is one of the most forbidding and desolate.

The Humboldt River is seen on our right as we pass through these alkali plains ; on our left are the towering peaks of the Humboldt mountains. The valley itself becomes more undulating, but still retains its dull monotony.

"Oreana" is soon reached, 400 miles from San Francisco. The descent from Humboldt has been quite rapid, and we will soon be at the lowest elevation in this great basin of sage brush and alkali.

Leaving "Oreana," we pass along a curve where the Humboldt River bends in toward the hills on our left, and soon cross the river, which makes its way into the Humboldt lake. The soil in this neighborhood is very rich, and if properly cultivated and well supplied with water, it would produce immense crops.

We next reach White Plains, 361 miles from San Francisco. This place is rightly named, for it is surrounded by a white alkali desert, covered in places with salt and alkali deposits.

The evidences of volcanic action, and a lava'formation, are everywhere visible in the hills and on the plains in the vicinity. Though the plains adjoining the station are white with alkali or salt deposits, yet the ridges and up- lands to the right are covered with the reddish porous rocks and blackish sand which always accompany this formation.

At White Plains we have reached the lowest elevation on the Central Pacific R. R., east of the Sierras. We are, in fact, almost in the sink itself of the Humboldt and Carson rivers. These two rivers flow into a large lake, called the Humboldt Sink, and it is plainly to be seen that this water sinks into the sand, for there are no out- lets to the sink.

Leaving White Plains, we begin to go up a grade, and are obliged to cross a divide between White Plains and Hot Springs Valley ; and this divide is reached at a place called "Mirage," 355 miles from San Francisco, and it is noted for the atmospheric forms seen there at certain times. When the atmosphere is favorable, visions of lakes, mountains, trees, rivers, and so forth, can be seen, and many a weary traveler has been deceived by the op- tical illusions that here seem so real, and wondered why he did not reach the cooling lakes and spreading shade, that seemed so near, yet was so far away.

The heat of summer on these plains is almost intolerable ; the dust blowing in clouds is suffocating, and, without water, one can easily imagine how tantalizing such visions must be to the weary traveler.

Crossing the low divide, in what may be called the terminus of the Antelope Range, we whirl away over a down grade, and in a few moments we arrive at "Hot Springs," 346 miles from San Francisco. Great efforts have been made here to sink Artesian wells, to obtain water for the engines and for the use of the railroad, but they have failed every time. Wells have been sunk over two thousand feet deep, but never reached water. In one day the drill went down over 95 feet, the next day less than one foot, and so on, but never reached any water, and that article has to be brought in pipes for many miles from the mountains. This station is named after certain hot springs near by, and can be seen from the cars as we pass along, and they are used by persons afflicted with skin diseases.

We leave this place, and are once more passing over the alkali plains or desert, and a more uninviting place than this we have not seen as yet.

We next come to a place called the Desert, 335 miles from San Francisco, and this place is rightly named.— The winds that sweep the barren plains here, keep the sand around the scattering sage-brush like huge potato hills. Now we turn toward the right, while boulders of lava, large and small, greet the eye. The hill on our left dwindles into a plain, we round toward the right, and arrive at "Two Miles." The gap in the mountains opens, and we see where the Truckee River comes tumbling down, and we are passing down a steep grade into the valley of the Truckee, where green grass grows, green trees and flowing water—God's best gift to man—again greets our vision. I wish to explain about this Humboldt river, which we have been following so long a time. It is over 500 miles long, and it has several tributaries constantly flowing into it, yet it does not increase in size as other rivers do. After passing Winemucca it diminishes to a small stream, and finally spreads to a mouth, and sinks out of sight.

We next come to a town, called Wadsworth, 328 miles from San Francisco. It is a little village nestling down in the valley of Truckee, and is overshadowed by a range of mountains beyond. Leaving Wadsworth, we cross the Truckee River, and gaze once more with delight upon trees, green meadows, comfortable homes, and well-tilled lands ; but, like every thing else lovely in this world, it soon fades from our view, as we rapidly pass into the "Truckee Cañon."

The mountains now come down on either side, as though they would shake hands across the silver torrent that divides them ; now the valley widens a little, then comes together again, and so we continue on our journey, and we hasten on, winding around promontories and in and out of ravines, through rocky cuts and over high embankments, with the river rolling and tumbling almost beneath our feet, and the ragged peaks towering high above us.

We soon come to a place called "Salvia," six miles below Wadsworth. Now we have something to occupy our attention ; new scenes are passing by at every length of the car, and we have to look sharp and quick, or many of them will be lost to our view. We soon turn to the right, and come to what the railroad men call Red Rock. Right in front, and hanging over our heads, is this large mountain of lava, thrown up out of the crater of some volcano in ages past ; and the shape and size of this rock is wonderful. I have not the language to express to you just how this monster appeared to me—it must be seen, then you can judge for yourself.

We next come to a station, called "Clarks," 313 miles from San Francisco. It is a beautiful place, with mountains all around it ; and the only way you see it, is by looking up toward the heavens.

Now we are at Vista, and we are going up-hill again.

and arrive at Truckee meadows. It is like an immense amphitheatre, and the traveler rejoices once more in seeing fine houses and cultivated fields, and scenes of beauty spread out before him.

We next come to Reno, where we leave the regular railroad line for the gold mines and Virginia City. But before saying anything about this route, and what followed, I wish to relate to you something about *letters*.

Receiving letters, or "letter-day," as it is called there. (Years ago letters were received only by the steamship, *via* the Isthmus, and, when steamer day comes, the whole population are in a state of excitement, and the day is celebrated by the firing of guns and ringing of bells, and an immediate rush for the Post-office. The delivery is principally from the window in the street, and a long line of anxious letter seekers is quickly formed, extending for a half mile down the street. Here are gathered the Gray Shirt Brigade of miners ; many of them have not had a line from home for over a year; next, anxious merchants, whose fate depended upon their getting their letters and invoices, and approaching the letter office, are dismayed at the extreme length of the line, with little hope of getting to the window for hours, and many of them offer large sums of money for a chance in the line near the window—for it takes half a day otherwise to get at the window—and there are lots of idlers, who have no friends, and who, of course, could not expect any letters, that would from pure mischief or love of speculation, take a place in the line. These men often make from $5 to $100 per day in this way, until it gets to be a common remark : "Selling out on the line ;" and many a loafer makes much money by this kind of trade. Men have been known to take their place in the line at least two days before the mail arrived, and just before the arrival of the steamship would be obliged to leave for a few moments, and on returning would be obliged to take their positions at the foot of the line.) And now we will return to our story, and, as I said before, we are now at Reno,

293 miles from San Francisco, in the Truckee mountains; and here we leave the regular railroad for Virginia City. We landed here on the 18th of April, and remained at the hotel over night, and the next morning, April 19th, at 7 o'clock, we took the train for the golden mines and the Big Bonanza.

We started on the crookedest road ever built by man. The whole length is 52 miles. A straight line across, from one end to the other is only 19 miles, so you see it must be a very crooked railroad, and it was on this road where the engineer saw one night a *red* light ahead of him. Supposing it was an engine coming down the track, he gave the alarm, " Down brakes," reversed the engine, and jumped off to save his life. And, lo and be- hold, it was the rear end of his own train ! I will not vouch for the truth of this story, but give it to you as I received it ; but I am ready to believe any stories that may be told me about this railroad, and I assure you it is a fact. We stopped at the " International Hotel," a new one, only 19 days old, and a splendid one it is too.— It is built on a side hill ; Virginia City is built also on a side hill, called the " Big Bonanza ;" the streets are cut into the hill, so that you can look down the chimneys of the houses on the street below you. After dinner we went down to the Ophir and Big Bonanza mines. In every direction are mines and shafts going down into the earth after gold and silver ; but the Ophir, and the Com- stock Big Bonanza mines are called the best and richest mines here, or anywhere else. We went to the Ophir mine (near the Big Bonanza) first, and found Mr. Com- stock, the head man in charge of both these mines. We had a letter of introduction to this gentleman, that satis- fied him we were all right. He took charge of us, and started for the shaft.

I asked my wife and Mrs. Gregory if they would ac- company me down the shaft, but both said very posi- tively " no, no !" On the contrary, my wife demanded of me all the ,money, tickets, watch, and everything about me that was of any value ; she then kissed me, shook hands, and bid me good bye—she had an idea that I would never come back alive. At first this rather staggered me, yet 1 thought I could go where other men could, so Frank, Mr. C. and myself went down, to see just what there was to be seen down in the mines. Mr. C. took us to a room, told us to change our clothes and put on miners' suits. We then stepped on to the shaft. A lantern was handed to each of us, and we took our position on the little cage, not over five feet square.

Mr. C. gave the signal to the engineer, and down we went. For the first few seconds I wished that I had remained on the surface of the earth, but in a very short time this feeling passed away. The cage is a heavy iron frame, with grooves on two sides, which fit upon wooden guides running from the top to the bottom of the mine. Upon these guides the cage runs smoothly through the whole course up and down the shaft, much the same as an elevator in a large hotel works.

The cage may have a single floor or platform, or it may have two or three floors or platforms, upon which cars of ore or other materials are placed. Those with two floors or platforms are called double-deckers, and the others three-deckers.

Mr. C. placed us, as I said before, on the cage, and showed us where we might safely grasp its iron form for support ; and as Mr. C. gets on board, and we are all in position, he gives the signal, and immediately we feel ourselves dropping into the depth and darkness of the shaft.

Our first thought was that between us and the bottom of the shaft, 2,000 feet below, was nothing but the frail platform of the cage, and instinctively we tighten our grip upon the iron bars of the cage, determined that should the bottom drop out, we will be found hanging to the upper works of our strange vehicle.

At the first plunge all is dark, but our lamps give a faint light, enough to see the sides of the shaft. Our view is very unsatisfactory, however, as all the timbers on the sides of the compartment appear to be darting swiftly upward, just as trees and telegraph poles do when we are going 40 miles an hour on a railroad ; our speed was probably not one half as fast as that, but we were satisfied not to go any faster.

In the early days of using this shaft, on receiving a "wink" from the foreman. the engine would drop down so fast that the men would have their breath almost taken away from them, but at present Mr. C. allows no such dangerous fooling. As we dart down the shaft, we soon begin to pass the stations of the first upper level ; our speed is such that we see but very little—we now and then get a glimpse of what appears to be a room of some size ; we see a few men standing about with lanterns in their hands, hear voices and the clank of machinery—an instant after all is smoothly sailing, and we see only the upward fleeing sides of the shaft ; then there is another place of many lights, glimpses of half-nude men, a number of voices, and a clash of machinery, and we have passed another station—it is like running past a railroad station in the night.

When we had descended about 1,500 feet we began to experience quite a novel sensation—that is the spring of the cable. Most persons have observed the very active bobbing motion of a toy ball suspended from an India-rubber string. The motion of our cage, hanging at the end of the cable, is much the same. The less one has of this peculiar motion the more he enjoys it. When this motion sets in, we at once begin to speculate in regard to the probable amount of stretch to be found in a first class steel wire cable, how far it may stretch before it reaches the breaking point. We are not, perhaps, over 500 feet from the bottom of the shaft, but we feel that we do not care to risk falling even that short distance.

However, should the cable really break, there would be no danger, for we should not fall. Attached to the upper part of the cage is a safety apparatus, designed especially to prevent accidents of this nature. At the instant that the cable parted there would be released powerful springs, which would throw out on each side of the shaft eccentric toothed wheels. These wheels, biting into the guides on each side, would instantly stop and hold the cage, block it fast in the shaft, and in case of the cable breaking, we should not fall an inch.

As we pass down the shaft, an occasional flash of light, a hum of voices, and a clash of machinery is heard, as described above.

Now the motion of the cage begins to slow, and a moment after we stop at a station 1,500 feet down below the surface, and we can hardly realize that we are so far from the upper world and daylight; but we have no time now to be philosophizing on our position, for we are now at the station.

I should say that there are levels every 100 feet; but this is a regular station, and here is the place for letting off passengers and taking on cars that are going up. This station is a large apartment, the walls of which are covered with rough boards, and the roof shows heavy supporting beams. Ranged along the walls of the station are boxes of candles, coils of fuse and many mining tools and stores; here is also a large cask of ice water. The ice is procured from above, while the water collects in the mine, as water is constantly running down the sides of the shaft.

The station is also a sort of lounging place, where the men who happen to have nothing to do for a few moments stop to hear the news from the surface; there is more chat and sociability here than in any other portion of the mine.

The reports of the stocks of the mines in San Francisco are sent to the miner at once, and about the time the report arrives, you will hear the men at the station anxiously inquiring the price of stocks of the first man who comes down from the surface. His report quickly passes through the mine, and very soon 600 or 700 men, far beneath the surface, know as much about the stocks of the mine as those who walk on the surface above.

Almost every miner owns some share in the mines, and there are men far down in the earth worth $40,000 or $50,000. and some of them worth much more. While at work they receive $4 per day, regularly, and they can speculate just as well as if they were on the streets watching the stock reports.

As I look, I see numerous avenues branching out from the station, like the ribs of a Chinese fan. Mr. C. took us through one of these, the longest, about three miles long. A car track is laid, and every few moments we were obliged to step on one side to let a mule pass, drawing one of the cars of ore to the station. These cars hold about 1,800 pounds of ore. Sometimes the cars are attended by men only, the mules being dispensed with.

In a few moments we find it is very warm, perspiration oozing from every pore, the sweat running in our boots. The miners are dressed very nearly after Adam and Eve's fashion, nothing on but a clout, or the waist of an old pair of pantaloons about their middle, a pair of shoes, and a hat—the hat to keep the fine particles of dust from the head, the clout to cover their middles, and the shoes to keep their feet from cutting on the sharp stones.

After seeing all there was to be seen, we retraced our steps to the station, and there we took a big iron box, called the "giraffe," and went down an inclined plane. This giraffe will hold 18 tons of ore. This inclined plane is over 600 feet long; and as we all tumbled into this iron box, the conductor gave the signal, and down we went. A strange feeling came over me at that time. The hole, or shaft, as it is called here, is not over six feet square, and on every side could be seen heavy timbers bracing up the ore and dirt from falling upon us; and as we got to the foot of this inclination, we find men nearly nude, and the perspiration running off them as if they had just come out of a river, shoveling ore into another giraffe, and at the same time heavy square pieces of timber are constantly being put up on the four sides, firmly held together. These were put up to keep the earth and ore from caving in upon us.

Way down there it is very hot, hotter than any place I was ever in before; but we did not seem to mind it at all. After seeing the sights, we tumbled into the giraffe again, ready to go—the conductor gave the signal—we were going up this time. Careful not to hit our heads against the beams, we lay down in the iron box on the top of the gold ore and dirt.

At the station we got out, took another good drink of ice water, and were ready to go up higher. Very soon we stepped aboard one of the cages, placed ourselves in position, the signal was given, and in a very short time, we once more stood in the cold air on the surface of the earth.

We found our friends waiting for us, and they appeared glad to again see us safe and sound; they acted as if we had just appeared from our graves. We shook hands with them, and then ran into a room prepared for us by Mr. C. It was a large bath room, with all the necessary accompaniments, hot and cold water, towels, and so forth. Immediately I was into it, taking a refreshing bath, and I think I never took one that did me more good than that one did. I should have mentioned that the bath man, who has charge of the costumes for going down into the mines, had considerable trouble in finding me a costume large enough. He finally hunted up Mr. Flood's—the rich man's costume—who is a large man. When dressed, I surveyed myself in a glass on the wall, but could get up no enthusiasm, though in wearing the clothes of a millionaire I thought I ought to have some feeling about it, but I would not scare worth a cent, and the feeling would not come. This Mr. Flood is worth over $80,000,000; and instead of being elated in my position, I felt as if it was old Boyer dressed in some body's else clothes. After taking a good look at myself I came out, and walked up

to my wife and introduced myself as a man worth $80,-
000,000; but she would not scare either—she thought the
jackass had put on the lion's skin only; and as I came
to the conclusion that she was right, I demanded of her
my trinkets. This extorted quite a laugh among the little crowd around us. Just then Mr. C. came to me, and
said that we had not got through yet. We stepped into
another room, and, lo and behold, there were all kinds
of liquors to drink, for the stomach's sake, as he said,
for it was a wet, nasty day outside, and not being used
to it I might catch cold. I tell you I never came so near
drinking as I did that day. But, Brothers, no! True to
my calling, in a very polite manner, I refused, and told
Mr. C. that I would take the chances on catching cold,
and the matter was dropped. After dressing, Mr. C. took
us into another room and showed us all the kinds of ore,
and also gave me a number of specimens of ore from
other mines. I should have said that, when down in the
mines, I shoveled up some ore into the giraffe, and also
put in my pocket a few pieces, and brought them home
for my friends to look at. Mr. C. said they came from a
mine worth $10,000 a ton when smelted. While shoveling
up the precious metals, it seemed to me like common
dirt; I was not overwhelmed a bit at the great work I
was performing.

After this Mr. C. took us into the inner office of the
rich men across the street, where only those are allowed
who have some extra business to attend to with the head
men. The reason why I was allowed there, was this:
I had shown Mr. C. my medal; he thought it something
wonderful—he was not an Odd Fellow, but a member of
the Masonic fraternity. Well, I could see him there,
too; but he was so taken up with my medal, that he
wanted me to show it to the richest man in the West, who
was a thorough working Odd Fellow. With the rest of
my family we called over to this office. We were ushered
into a room; I wish I could give a description of it; but
let me say it was all that money could make it or art

suggest. We waited a little for the head man; soon he came, and I was introduced to him—Mr. John Mackay by name, a Scotchman, one of the original owners of the Big Bonanza. He formerly kept a common rum-hole in San Francisco, where he located in 1849, a very poor man, and to-day he is worth over $80,000,000. He looked at my medal, and then looked at me. What he thought I don't know, but what he said I recollect well enough, something like this : "That is a very nice medal you have, and I presume you appreciate it as such." I found he was able to talk on Odd Fellowship, and we had quite a chat on that subject.

I will mention just here that there were four men who originally owned the Big Bonanza, and had I the time to write and you the patience to hear me, I think it would prove a very interesting story to tell you all about these four men in the early days of this mine, years ago ; but to-day they are worth many, many millions of dollars. Their names are Mackay, Fair, Flood, and O'Brien. Their united yearly income is over $20,000,000.

I wish to say a word about the production of the Big Bonanza. For more than a year it has yielded over $1,800,000 a month, and there is no sign of exhaustion yet. In 1875, and four months of 1876, this mine yielded over $25,000,000. In the month of March, 1876, they took out over $4,000,000 in bullion ; and much more could be said about this wonderful mine, but I will defer it to some other time.

We shook hands with our new friends, and then started for the hotel, had our dinner, and got ready to start for Reno. Three o'clock came, Mrs. Gregory, my wife and myself started down the hill for the depot, two blocks away, we got on board—the time came for our departure, but no Frank could be found. I spoke to the conductor, and told him how I was fixed. He waited five minutes to give me time to send up to to the Hotel and hunt up "that boy;" but no tidings of him could be had. The train started, and upon getting to the foot of the street leading up to the hotel, I looked up, and there was Frank coming down full split in the middle of the street, mud flying, and the *boy too*. I asked the brakeman to stop the train, and he replied that he dared not do it ; I wanted to know the reason why ? his answer was that the train was going down a steep grade, and the cars could not stop ; I replied that I would do it myself, and I did it. I never in all my life pulled a rope as I did then, and in a few minutes the cars stopped—I ran back to the rear end of the train ; Frank had got there by that time, but was too weak to get on board. I pulled him up on the platform, and we entered the car, when the conductor came rushing back and wanted to know who dared to stop the train ; I owned right up, and pointed to Frank—he was the cause of it, I said, and I wanted to know if I could give a better answer than the one before him ; said I, just look at him, mud from head to foot, and looking more like a drowned rat than any thing else—and, said I, why don't you go on now ? what are you waiting for ? And I was upon the point of pulling the bell-rope, to start the train again, when the conductor saw my movement, and pulled the rope himself, and at the same time I heard him muttering something about somebody having more brass than, &c., &c., &c., but I didn't care. Once more we were going down this steep grade and around sharp curves, and finally got down to the valley all right, and arrived at Reno safe and sound, at 9 P. M., April the 19th, ready to start westward once more.

LECTURE NO. 4.

But, before resuming the account of our trip, I want
to tell you about flumes.

THE GREAT NEVADA FLUME.

A PERILOUS RIDE.

A fifteen mile ride in a flume down the Sierra Nevada
mountains, in 35 minutes, was not one of the things con-
templated on my visit to Virginia City, and it is entirely
within reason to say that I shall never make the trip
again.

The flume cost, with its appurtenances, between $200,-
000 and $300,000. It was built by a company interested
in the mines here, principally owners of the Consolidated
Virginia, California, Hale & Norcross, Gould & Curry,
Best & Belcher, and Utah mines. The largest stock-
holders are J. C. Flood, James G. Fair, John Mackay,
and W. S. O'Brien, the wealthiest firm in the United
States.

The mines named use 1,000,000 feet of lumber per month,
underground, and burn 40,000 cords of wood per year.
Wood here is worth from $10 to $12 per cord, and at
market prices, Messrs. Flood & Co. would have to pay,
for wood alone, nearly $500,000 per year.

Virginia City is not built in a forest. From the top of
Mount Davidson, which is half a mile back from the
city, there is not a tree in sight, except a few shade trees
in the city.

Going into the mines, the other day, and seeing the
immense amount of timber used, I asked Mr. Mackay
where all the wood and timber came from ; " It comes,"
said he, "from our lands in the Sierras, forty or fifty

miles from here ; we own over 12,000 acres in the vicinity of Washoe Lake, all of which is heavily timbered."

" How do you get it here ?" I asked.

" It comes," said he, " in our flume down the mountains, 15 miles, and from our dumping grounds is brought by the Virginia and Truckee Railroad to this city, sixteen miles. You ought to see this flume before you go back, it is really a wonderful thing."

The Journey.—When, therefore, two days afterward, I was invited to accompany Mr. Flood and Mr. Fair to the head of the flume, I did not hesitate to accept their kind offer. We started at four o'clock in the morning, in two buggies ; the two gentlemen named in one buggy, and Mr. Hereford, the President and Superintendent of the Company (which is known as the Pacific Wood, Lumber and Flume Company), and myself in the other.

The drive through the Washoe Valley, and along the mountains, up and down for 16 miles, over a road which, for picturesqueness. is without an equal in memory, cannot be described. Not a tree, nor bush, nor any green vegetation was in sight ; hills and mountains, well-defined and separate in character, were in every direction. Sagebrush and jack rabbits were the only living things in sight. That beautiful purple atmosphere, or mist, which has a dreamy, sleepy effect in the landscape, overspread the mountains, and extended through the valley.

The road we traversed swung round and round the mountains, now going nearly to the summit, and now descending to their base.

Both teams employed were of the best, and in less than an hour and a half we had accomplished the first part of our journey, 16 miles. Here we breakfasted, and went to the end of the flume, a quarter of a mile distant. The men were running timber, 16 inches square and ten feet long, through it. The tressle work, upon which the flume rested, was about 20 feet from the ground. The velocity of the movement of the timber could scarcely be credited, for it requires from only twenty-five minutes to half an hour for it to float the entire length of the flume, 15 miles.

The flume is shaped like the letter V, and is made of 10-inch plank nailed together in the above shape. Across the top it is about two and one-half feet in width. The ends are very carefully fitted so that where the planks go together there may be no unevenness, for timbers going at the rate of 15 to 60 miles per hour must have a clear coast. In this trough the water runs from Hunter's Creek, which is situated about twenty miles from the terminus of the flume. Some idea of the swiftness with which the timber runs through the flume may be had when it is stated that in the flume there floats 500,000 feet of lumber every day (about 10 hours), or 500 cords of wood. Near the terminus an iron break is placed in the trough, slanting toward one side, so that when the timber comes rushing down, 50 or 100 pieces, one after the other, each piece is turned toward the side and the men at the break, with a dexterous use of the crowbar, send them bounding to the ground. I climbed to the top of the tressle work before the timber began to come. It was like the rushing of a herd of buffalo, or a party of hunters, and I preferred to view the flume in active working from a safe distance.

We changed teams upon resuming our journey, taking fresh horses for the mountain ascent. Horsemen in the East, who have never seen the mountains of Nevada, Colorado and California, can have no idea of the amount of work a horse can do and of the difficult places through which he will go and of the load he will carry or draw. How a pair of horses can pull a buggy and two men up a grade that seems half-way between the horizontal and perpendicular, over stones and fallen trees, and through underbrush six feet high and very thick, is a question I can never hope to solve; at any rate, we reached the lower mill of the Company, about 18 or 20 miles. This was several hours before noon. The mill is situated in the lower belt of timber, and there are between 400 and 500 men at work. This number includes those engaged in cutting trees, hauling logs and sawing the lumber. How the heavy machinery of the mills, and the engines that work them, were brought from the city up the mountains and placed in position, is another mystery which I have not tried to investigate.

The amount of lumber turned out by the owner of these mills, the upper and the lower, the former being two and a half miles farther up the mountain, is marvellous. In five minutes' time, a log from two to four feet in diameter, is reduced to lumber, planks, scantling, boards and square timber, perhaps all from the same log, for it is cut in the most advantageous manner. Sometimes one log will give three or four kinds of lumber. The lower mill is kept running night and day, and has a capacity of 50,000 feet per day of small stuff, and of 70,000 feet when working on large timber. The upper mill has less than half the capacity, being smaller, and being worked only 12 hours a day.

The Flume.—The flume is a wonderful piece of engineering work. It is built wholly upon tressle work and stringers: there is not a cut in the whole distance, and the grade is so heavy there is little danger of a jam. The tressle work is very substantial, and is undoubtedly strong enough to support a narrow gauge railway. It runs over foot-hills, through valleys, around mountains, and across cañons. In one place it is 70 feet high. The highest point of the flume from the plain is 3,700 feet, and on an air line, from beginning to end, the distance is eight miles, the course thus taking up 7 miles in twists and turns; the tressle work is thoroughly braced, longitudinally across, so that no break can extend further than a single box, which is 16 feet; all the main supports, which are five feet apart, are firmly set in mud-sills, and the boxes or troughs rest in brackets four feet apart; these again rest upon substantial stringers. The grade of the flume is between 1,600 and 2,000 feet from the top to the lower end, a distance of 15 miles.

The sharpest fall is three feet in six. There are two reservoirs from which the flume is fed. One is 1,600 feet long and the other 600 feet; a ditch nearly two miles long takes the water to the first reservoir, whence it is conveyed 3½ miles to the flume through a feeder capable of carrying 450 inches of water. The whole flume was built in ten weeks. In that time all the tressle work, stringers and boxes were put in place. About 200 men were employed on it at one time, being divided into four gangs. It required 2,000,000 feet of lumber, but the item which astonished me most was that there were 28 tons, or 56,000 pounds, of *nails* used in the construction of this flume.

To the lower mill, as the road goes, it is about 40 miles to Virginia City. Although I had already ridden this distance, yet I mounted a horse and rode two or three miles to the top of the mountain, where I had one of the finest valley views that comes to the lot of man. Miles and miles below the valley was spread out, with spots and squares of green crops growing, and barren wastes of sand and sage-brush, reaching in a long stretch to the base of another spur of the Sierras.

The city of Reno occupied a little spot on the plain. From my mountain it seemed like a city of toy houses built on nature's carpet.

A Ride in the Flume.—Upon my return I found that Mr. Flood and Mr. Fair had arranged for a ride in the flume, and I was challenged to go with them. Indeed, the proposition was put in the form of a challege—they dared me to go. I thought that if men worth $25,000,000 or $30,000,000 apiece could afford to risk their lives, I could afford to risk mine, which was not worth half so much. So I accepted the challenge, and two *boats* were ordered. These were nothing more than pig troughs with one end knocked out. The "boat" is built, like the flume, V shaped, and fits into the flume. It is composed of three pieces of wood, two two-inch planks 16 feet long, and an end board, which is nailed about 2½ feet across the top.

The forward end of the boat was left open, the rear end left closed with a board, against which was to come the current of water to propel us. Two narrow boards were placed in the boat for seats, and everything was made ready. Mr. Fair and myself were to go in the first boat, and Mr. Flood and Mr. Hereford in the other.

Mr. Fair thought we had better take a third man with us who knew something about the flume. There were probably 50 men from the mill standing waiting to see us off, and when it was proposed to take a third man, the question was asked of them if anybody was willing to go. Only one man, a red-faced carpenter, who takes more kindly to whisky than his bench, volunteered to go.

Finally, everything was arranged. Two or three stout men held the boat over the flume and told us to jump into it the minute it touched the water, and to "*hang on to our hats.*"

The signal of "*all ready*" was given, the boat was launched, and we jumped into it as best we could, which was not very well, and away we went like the wind. One man who helped to launch the boat fell into it just as the water struck it, but he scampered out on the tressle, and whether he was hurt or not we could not wait to see. The grade of the flume at the mill is very heavy, and the water rushes through it at railroad speed.

The terrors of that ride can never be blotted from the memory of one of that party. To ride upon the cow-catcher of an engine down a steep grade is simply exhilarating, for you know there is a wide track, regularly laid upon a firm foundation; that there are wheels grooved and fitted to the track; that there are trusty men at the brakes, and, better than all, you know that the power that impels the train can be rendered powerless in an instant by the driver's light touch upon his lever. But a flume has no element of safety. In the first place, the grade cannot be regulated as it can upon a railroad; you cannot go fast or slow at pleasure; you are wholly at the mercy of the water; you cannot stop, you cannot lessen your speed; you have nothing to hold to; you have only to sit still, shut your eyes, say your prayers, take all the water that comes—filling your boat, wetting your feet, drenching you like a plunge through the surf—and wait for eternity. It is all there is to hope for after you are launched in a flume boat. I cannot give the reader a better idea of a flume ride than to compare it to riding down an old-fashioned eave trough at an angle of 45 degrees, hanging in mid-air without support of roof or house, and thus shot a distance of 15 miles. At the start we went at the rate of 20 miles an hour, which is a little less than the average speed of a railroad train. The reader can have no idea of the speed we made till he compares it to a railroad. The average time we made was 30 miles an hour, a mile in two minutes, for the entire distance. This is greater than the average running time of railroads.

Incidents of the Ride.—The red faced carpenter sat in front of our boat, on the bottom, as best he could. Mr. Fair sat on a seat behind him, and I sat behind Mr. Fair in the stern, and was of great service to him 'in keeping the water, which broke over the end-board, from his back.

There was a great deal of water also, shipped in the bows of the hog-trough, and I know Mr. Fair's broad shoulders kept me from many a wetting in that memorable trip.

At the heaviest grade the water came in so furiously in front, that it was impossible to see where we were going, or what was ahead of us ; but when the grade was light, and we were going at a four-minute pace, the vision was very delightful, although it was terrible.

In this ride, which fails me to describe, I was perched up in a boat no wider than a chair, sometimes twenty feet high in the air, and with the ever varying altitude of the flume often seventy feet high. When the water would enable me to look ahead I would see this trestle here and there for miles, so small and narrow, and appa-

rently so fragile, that I could only compare it to a chalk
mark, upon which, high in the air, I was running at a rate
unknown upon railroads.

One circumstance during the trip did more to show me
the terrible rapidity with which we dashed through the
flume, than anything else. We had been rushing down
at a pretty lively rate of speed when the boat suddenly
struck something in the bow—a nail, or lodged stick of
wood—which ought not to have been there. What was the
result? The red faced carpenter was sent whirling into
the flume, ten feet ahead. Fair was precipitated on his
face, and I found a soft lodgment on Fair's back.

It seemed to me that in a second's time, Fair, himself
a powerful man, had the carpenter by the scruff of the
neck and had pulled him into the boat. I did not know
that, at this time, Fair had his fingers crushed between
the boat and the flume.

But we sped along; minutes seemed hours. It
seemed an hour before we arrived at the worst place in
the flume, and yet Hereford tells me it was less than ten
minutes. The flume, at the point alluded to, must have
very near 45 degrees inclination. In looking out before
we reached it, I thought the only way to get to bottom
was to fall. How our boat kept in the track is more
than I know. The wind, the steamboat, the railroad,
never went so fast. I have been where the wind blew at
the rate of eighty miles an hour, and yet my breath was
not taken away. In the flume, in the bad places, it
seemed as if I would suffocate. The first bad place that
we reached, and if I remember right, it was the worst, I
got close to Fair. I did not know that I would survive
the journey, but I wanted to see how fast we were going.
So I lay close to him and placed my head between his
shoulders. The waters were coming into his face like
the breakers of the ocean. When we went slow the
breakers came in on my back, but when the heavy
grades were reached, the breakers were in front. In
one case Fair shielded me, and in the other I shielded
Fair.

In this particularly bad place I allude to, my desire was to form some judgment of the speed we were making. If the truth must be spoken, I was almost scared out of reason ; but if I was on the way to eternity, I wanted to know how fast I went ; so I huddled close to Fair and turned my eyes towards the hills. Every object I placed my eyes on was gone, before I could clearly see what it was. Mountains passed like visions and shadows. It was with difficulty that I could get my breath. I felt that I did not weigh one hundred pounds, although I knew in the sharpness of intellect which one has at such a moment, that the scales turned at *two hundred.*

Mr. Flood and Mr. Hereford, although they started several minutes later than we did, were close upon us. They were not so heavily loaded, and they had the full sweep of the water, while we had it rather at second-hand. Their boat finally struck ours with a terrible crash.

Mr. Flood was thrown upon his face, and the waters flowed over him, leaving not a dry thread upon him. What became of Hereford I do not know, except that when he reached the terminus of the flume he was as wet as any of us.

This only remains to be said, we made the entire distance in less time than a railroad train would ordinarily make, and a portion of the time we went faster than a railroad train ever went. Fair said that we went at least a mile a minute. Flood said we went at the rate of 100 miles and hour, and *my* deliberate belief is that we went at a rate that annihilated time and space. We were a wet lot when we reached the terminus of the flume. Flood said he would not make the trip again for the whole *Consolidated Virginia Mines.* Fair said that he should never again place himself on an equality with timber and wood, and Hereford said he was sorry that he ever built the flume. As for myself, I told the millionaire that I had accepted my last challenge. When we left our boats we were more dead than alive. We had yet 16 miles to drive to Virginia City. How we reached

home the reader will never know. I asked Flood what I
was to do with my spoiled English clothes. He bade me
good-night, with the remark that my clothes were good
enough to give away. The next day, neither Flood nor
Fair were able to leave their beds. For myself, I had
only strength enough left to say, "*I have had enough
of Flumes.*"

We will now resume our journey from Reno westward,
and we do not stop again until our arrival at Sacramento,
139 miles from San Francisco, at 8 o'clock in the morning of the 20th of April.

The population of this city is about 20,000, and it is
the capital of the State of California. Many objects of
great interest might be mentioned about this city, but
we must be excused, and hurry on to San Francisco.
After breakfast we started and took the cars to Vallejo,
where we made connection with the steamboat running
down the Sacramento bay into the great bay of San
Francisco, where we arrived at the end of our journey,
at 10 o'clock A. M. We took a carriage for the largest
hotel in the world—so said to be by those who claim to
know—called the Palace Hotel ; only seven stories high,
has five elevators in it, a large court, where you drive
right inside ; but no business is done on the sidewalk
outside of the building. This property was built by or
for Mr. Ralston, who committed suicide. The building
was then turned over to Senator Sharon. The original
cost of this great structure was $7,000,000, bought in for
less than one quarter of this sum by Senator Sharon.

It is now run by Warren Leland, one of the Leland
Brothers of New York. I have a number of photographs
of this great building. In the evening I attended a
Lodge of Odd Fellows, at Odd Fellows' Hall ; not knowing one from the other, I strolled into the first one I came
to ; it turned out to be a French Lodge. I was introduced, through my card. I found P. G. Preston, of Atlantic Lodge, there, ahead of me ; for he started a week
before I did from New York. We did not stay long at

the French Lodge, although while there I became acquainted with P. G. Day's nephew, who went out there years ago. He was at the Lodge, in company with the D. D. G. Master of that district, to get this French Lodge to sign a petition for him to start a new Lodge, to be called Morse Lodge, named after our lamented Brother Morse, of this Lodge, years ago, who died some time since.

After a little we retired, and visited San Francisco Lodge, across the Hall, where we had a very interesting time.

April 21st, in company with P. G. Preston, who seemed to know all about this town, having lived here in 1854, I strolled around through the town. We called upon D. G. Sire Farnsworth, and found him a gentleman of the first water, his head full of business, and at the same time would and could talk about Odd Fellowship. We also called upon Brother Austin, editor of the " New Age," an Odd Fellows' paper, and P. G. R. Nathan Porter. Both these men are what you may call real live Odd Fellows, rich men with many dollars, but always ready to say and to do something for our cause. They seemed to have the interests of Odd Fellowship at heart. We called upon other brothers, for I had letters of introduction to all the principal Odd Fellows of San Francisco, and found them men of culture, smart, alive and ready to do something to advance our cause ; I might say I was treated right cordially, and invited to make my home with them while in town. Of course. I thanked them for their kindness, but I preferred to remain with my family at the hotel.

During the day P. G. Preston took me to that particular quarter of the city called Chinese Town. Now, I wish I could tell you in a few words what we saw there ; but language fails me, the heathen Chinee must be studied to be understood. Once in a while you will see one or more of the male sex promenading the streets ; but go to San Francisco, and see all kinds and classes, men, women and children, all huddled in three or four narrow streets, 40,000 of them, down in dark cellars or up in garrets, actually swarming like bees, 15 or 20 occupying a room not more than fifteen feet square.— Many of them laying on shelves hung around in the room, and then the women, with all their cheap jewelry, always, when in the street, wearing a string of keys and other things hanging from their waists. They have very very little feet, and, as a class, are very small in stature in comparison with the women of other countries. They are quick to learn, are inveterate smokers, also great gamblers, and have other vices not necessary to mention at this time. In company with my family, I visited their Joss House (a church), and witnessed their Chistian services, as they term it. Nothing like it can be seen in any other country, except China itself. They worship gods stuck up on every bench—they know nothing about a true God ; their god is called "Joss," a wooden image, and nothing more. We remained and saw them go through with their heathenish service, which was sickening in the extreme, and must be seen to be appreciated.

Chinese die, and are buried like other folks, but their burial service is entirely different. I will describe what took place at one funeral while we were there. A Chinaman, called Long John Khar, a Chinese merchant doing business at 911 Dupont Street, right in the middle of the Chinese quarters, was buried with great ceremonies.— Early in the forenoon the body was placed in a room, and surrounded by about twenty women, who were employed as mourners. They were dressed in white capes, with white bands about their heads, and they sway back and forth in unison, keeping up a continual howling, crying and moaning.

At 12 M. the body was taken to a platform which had been erected before the house, and further ceremonies were performed. A large number of roasted pigs and loaves of cake were placed about the coffin, and strips of paper, bearing mystical signs, were thrown upon the body. The whole platform was surrounded by burning candles, two of the Chinese bands were playing funeral marches, while among the crowds which packed the street from Washington Street to Jackson, a man scattered small coins, which were carefully done up in tinted paper. The coffin was an elegant silver-bound casket, with the name of the deceased beautifully engraved on a silver plate.

From thence to the grave, upon Lone Mountain Hill, where all classes and denominations have their burying places, the women still followed the body, keeping up their howling and crying as they went along. The pigs and loaves of cake were in a wagon next to the hearse, and they were placed upon the surface of the grave and around it. The Chinese watch their graves, so that the hoodlums shall not steal their pigs and cake from the grave. After a while all is gone, but no one knows where or how.

On Saturday night, September 21st, I attended an encampment of Odd Fellows, called the Oriental Encampment. They had six candidates for the Royal Purple degree. I have never witnessed the work done as it was that night. There were six candidates and six guides, a guide for each candidate, and the first two were handled exceedingly rough.

And talk about riches! Why, one candidate was represented to me as being worth $200,000 or so. The guide alongside of him was worth $500,000, or half a million, and the Junior Warden over $1,000,000, and many members in the room were represented to me as being worth much more money, even beyond calculation. I spent a very pleasant evening, and returned home at 11½ P. M.

On Sunday, April 22d, I went to Dr. Stone's Congregational Church, one of the leading churches of San Francisco The text was from Galatians vi. 14: "But God forbid that I should glory, save in the cross of our Lord Jesus Christ."

In the afternoon we all went to Woodward's Garden, kept by a live Odd Fellow, by the name of Woodward.

The sights seen there are wonderful beyond description, and we spent a happy afternoon, came home, took tea, and spent the evening in writing letters home and elsewhere.

Monday, April 23d, I spent the forenoon in taking a carriage ride with my family, and went about ten miles out to see the Cliff House on the Pacific Coast. Went through, near the Golden Gate;—the beautiful Park, built on great heaps of sand, called the Golden Gate Park, which extends from the city westward over hills of sand to the Pacific Ocean, some ten miles. Here we found, at the entrance to the Golden Gate, a number of very high rocks off in the ocean, 500 feet or more from shore. These high rocks are always covered with an innumerable number of sea lions, and can be seen very distinctly with a marine spy-glass. With the roaring of the surf, and the still louder roaring of these wonderful animals, the sight and noise is extraordinary.

I undertook to count the animals lodged on one side of a rock only, but I failed, for they are seldom still, long enough to count them. The whole island appears to be covered with these animals, rolling and tumbling over each other, and all trying to get upon the rocks high enough to be able to lay still for a few minutes.

While looking very intently at a great big lion, black as coal, coming out of the water, I noticed a general getting away of the other lions giving the black monster room to get up. Pretty soon he reached where he seemed to be at home, and laid down to have a sleep; but soon, from the other side of the rock, the lions would punch him with their noses, and this would cause him to open his mouth. And such a yell ! All the Comanche Indians in the West could not hold a candle in this hallooing to him. When he opened his mouth it appeared as if he could swallow a horse or a cow, for it appeared as large as a cart wheel.

On inquiry, I found that this monster was an old favorite among the sea lions, and his name was "Ben Butler." I am no great judge of weight, but this sea lion is estimated to weigh over 7,000 pounds. I tried to discover a "*stye in his eye*," but failed to discover one, and therefore I am at a loss to know why he is called "Ben Butler," for he does not look like him, nor in any way does he resemble that honorable statesman.

After watching these wonderful animals a while, we went to the Odd Fellows' cemetery, about five miles from the city. I traced my steps to P. G. M. Morse's grave, took some flowers from off it and brought them home; but they did not live, although I kept them alive till within two hundred miles of my home.

I should have said that we went to the Cliff House, built where a good view of the sea lions and seals could be obtained ; and from its piazza, we, with many others, witnessed the playful actions of these animals.

After viewing the Masonic and other cemeteries, we went to our hotel, very well pleased with our forenoon amusement, then had our dinner, and spent the rest of the day in seeing the sights in the city. In the evening I went to California Lodge, the one to which brother Morse belonged while living in this city. I was much edified during the evening, and came away well pleased with my visit.

Thursday, April 24th, my family went to Sacramento, to be gone a day or two, so that I was left to roam about. In the morning I went to the Masonic Temple, and was introduced to brothers of the order. The Janitor took me through the entire building.

In the evening I attended a Veteran Odd Fellows meeting, an association of Odd Fellows who have been in the order over twenty years, at Odd Fellows Hall. The object of this association is to create a new society, and their idea is to have a good time every three months, visit the lodges in the neighborhood, give them good advice, help them on in the good cause, generally feed the fires of Odd Fellowship, and keep them burning upon the altar of every true Odd Fellow's heart. This meeting organized by electing Brother N. Porter, as President; and other work was done. Over 150 members responded to the call ; and all those who had been Odd Fellows over twenty years were entitled to membership.

April 25th was spent in visiting sundry places. The first place was the Mission Church. This is one of the institutions of the city, and is over 100 years old, of the old Spanish rite kind. Services are held every day. The old lamp is kept burning over the altar as it was one hundred years ago. This church has three bells hung over the entrance to the church, and every day in the year, at 12 noon, these bells are rung. In the rear of the church is the grave yard. On walking through it, I came across Yankee Sullivan's grave. It will be recollected that this Yankee Sullivan was a great fighter. In the year 1856, he, among others of his kind, had been seized by the Vigilance Committee, tried, and convicted of the many crimes charged, and sentenced to banishment. While awaiting the arrival of the vessel which was to convey the cargo of human scum from the shores California, confined in one of the cells of the Vigilante's building, on Commercial Street, he learned that William Mulligan, his deadly enemy, of whom he stood in mortal dread, would be one of his companions on the trip ; he thereupon sharpened the table-knife with which he cut his food, and then haggled his left arm, above the elbow, with this knife, in such a manner as to cause his death. His true name was James Sullivan.

I also visited the mint, a great institution, the largest of its kind in the world. They have milled over $3,000,-000 a day.

In the evening I visited Templar Lodge, the one to which Bros. Porter and Farnsworth belong. I find the work about on a par with old Atlantic. They had no initiation, but they had a subject to talk about that instructed the brethren pretty well. It was this : " Should the Trustees go on and finish putting up grave-stones, of a proper kind, to each of the brothers buried in their lot, or not, as they were instructed to do some two years ago."

The Trustees hesitated to go on putting up the stones as they had been directed to do two years before, and had decided in their own minds to have another vote from the lodge before doing so. After a lengthy discussion, the vote was taken, and they were directed to go on at once and finish up the job, and to do what they were told to do. After some other business, the Lodge closed, and I returned to my hotel.

April 26th. This is the 58th anniversary of our Order in the United States, and the Odd Fellows of San Francisco decided to have a pic-nic on the occasion, at a place called Belmont, some thirty miles from here, on the Southern Pacific Railroad.

A great crowd of men, women and children, gathered, the number being estimated at 30,000 on the grounds at one time. Nothing occurred to break the harmony of the great meeting, unless the falling of the dance-room floor, by which a number of ladies and children were hurt, some pretty badly. The programme was curious, and consisted of music, singing, dancing, spelling, running races, chasing a greased pig, and so on, and wound up nicely. In the evening we returned home, and I found that my wife had returned home from Sacramento all right.

April 27. Spent this day, in company with my family, in sight-seeing at different places. We visited the mint again, and saw money, money, money, everywhere laying loose on the floor, on shelves, and in boxes; many thousand dollars of gold were spread out before us. We returned home, and had for dinner all kinds of vegetables, peas, beans, strawberries, &c.,—and recollect this was only the 27th of April; in fact, we had every kind of garden truck that is generally raised in hothouses; but here it is different, all of this produce grows in the open air.

April 28—Saturday. This day was spent in seeing the sights, and in the afternoon we went to Oakland, which is to San Francisco the same as Brooklyn is to New York.

We take a ferry-boat, and go about two miles to a pier two miles in length, the longest pier ever built by man, and then take the cars for Oakland. After seeing Oakland (which takes its name from the beautiful live oaks all through and around it), we went to Brooklyn, some two miles back from Oakland.

I asked the driver if he knew all about Brooklyn. He said he did ; I then told him to drive to 399 Clinton Street, my home in Brooklyn. He thought for a moment, and finally said I had him, for there was no such place in Brooklyn ; I differed with him, and told him that that was my home. He soon saw the joke, and drove on.

I notice many scrub oak trees, and at a distance they look very much like apple trees ; they are not very large or tall ; the trunk may be 8 or 10 feet high, and then they spread out, and have very hard limbs. We saw very beautiful houses and grounds everywhere. Oakland and Brooklyn, out here, appear to be the retiring places for the merchants and others of San Francisco. After spending a very pleasant afternoon we returned home.

In the evening I attended a Rebecca degree Lodge, called the Templar Lodge, No. 19, and was well entertained while there.

April 29—Sunday. In the morning went to Plymouth Congregational Church, F. K. Noble, pastor, and a noble man he is, too. He preached from Matthew iv., 10, 11, about the devil tempting Christ, and a splendid sermon it was. In the evening, went to hear Chaplain McCabe preach, at the Howard St. M. E. Church. He preached on church extension. After the services, the chaplain sung a number of his sweet songs of praise ; and a most delightful singer the chaplain is. I heard him here, in Brooklyn, soon after the war closed ; I did not see that he had lost much of his old style of singing. This Chaplain was in the Union army, was captured, and sent to Libby prison, and was there many months.

April 30. Spent this day in fixing up things generally. I called on Mr. Joseph W. Wynant, President of the

Society for Prevention of Cruelty to Animals, and he appeared right glad to see one who belonged to the Parent Society in New York. He introduced me to his Secretary, in another part of the building, and made me promise to call again before I returned to Brooklyn; but I was so busy that I was prevented from doing so. In the evening went down to the steamboat landing, and met Mrs. Gregory returning home from her brother's in Sacramento. Escorted the lady to her hotel, and spent the rest of the evening with my family.

May 1. This day spent in getting ready to go to the Geysers. Started at 2½ P. M., took steamboat named the "James M. Donevan," for Donahue, thence by cars to Cloverdale, and arrived there, and remained over night. We stopped at the only hotel in the village, kept by a Dutchman. The hotel was full, and the landlord owned a cottage near by; he offered to give us the cottage during the night to sleep in, in words something like these : "Mine hodell is ferry vull, and I dinks you all hat petter gum ofer the gottage, vare you will pe all py yournsefes, for it is petter vor old peobles vat vants to schleeps, day hat petter pe py temselves vare dare is no noise." So ve old peobles vent ore mit de gottage, vare ve could have it ferry schtill, so ve could schleeps. On arriving at the cottage we found it splendidly furnished, with an organ in the parlor. We had Sanckey's book of hymns, Mrs. Gregory and Mr. Marsh and wife, from Brooklyn, in company with us commenced singing, and such a time as we had altogether, in singing, telling stories, &c., &c. ; why the people in the hotel proper did not know what to make of it ; the neighbors collected together, and they inquired of the landlord what was going on at the cottage. He replied by saying a lot of "beoples, vat vas old beoples," had taken the cottage to schleep in, and he daut dey vas only schnoring a very little. The answer was satisfactory, and we, seven persons, will never forget the night at the cottage in Cloverdale.

May 2. We took a four-horse stage for the Geysers, early in the morning, a distance of eighteen miles. The first four miles of this route runs through the beautiful Russian Valley, where we saw fields of wheat, and other kinds of grain in great abundance. We then commenced to ascend the mountains, winding hither and thither along the sides of the foot of the hills, often under the wide-spreading oak and other trees ; sometimes descending a little, then rising higher and higher, until we reach the great "Hogs' Back," or crowning ridge. The scene from this point, looking backward, is a grand one, whose beauty no pen can adequately describe. The morning is bright, the air is still, every breath of this pure mountain air is laden with an inspiration of thought. Away in the blue distance the ocean can be seen ; near by, and almost beneath us, are seen the green fields, the trees on plain and hillside, from the cone and bower-like form to that of the straight and spirit-like pine and fir tree, dot-ting the landscape with emeralds, making the whole sur-prisingly beautiful.

Wild flowers, of the most beautiful kind, are strewn over the mountains, and the blossoms of the "Buck-Eye" and the mountain lilac perfume the air, while the birds break the silence with their songs.

At the bottom of a beautiful "Cañon," darkly shaded with trees, was a large mountain stream, at which we all got out, watered our horses, and rested ourselves. After a short rest we started again ; and from this place we descended very rapidly—some 1,900 feet, in a distance of but two miles—and as we would come around some sharp point, the leaders of our team often out of sight on the other side of the ridge, we would involuntarily shut our eyes and hold our breath (as we supposed we would, were we dropping from the skies) ; and thus for two hours did we fly through this mountain gorge. At 10 A. M. we dropped, as it were, in front of our hotel, called the Geyser Springs Hotel, and we all took a good long breath, thanking God for our safe deliverance.

The Great Geysers are directly in front of us, on the other side of the "Gorge" or "Cañon" as it is called here. This "Geyser Cañon," is quite narrow at its junction with the creek, but widens gradually as it ascends.

We, in company with our guide, at 4 P. M., left the hotel, passed through a gate down a path leading to "Pluton's Creek." Here we passed over a rustic bridge, then followed a trail. We soon reached the Geyser stream of warm water, which cascades over craggy rocks into a deep gorge, completely shaded by a dense growth of box or laurel trees.

The first thing that attracted our attention was the "Eye-water Spring." I have a vial of the same for exhibition here this evening. The next point is the "Devil's Office," a weird grotto-like place, with crystals of Epsom salts hanging from its rocky banks. The guide is particular in giving the name of each place, as being associated with the devil. We will leave out his satanic majesty's name pretty generally, and note each point of attraction as we ascend the cañon, in their order. From this upward, as we climb the cañon, there are no trees or vegetation. This cañon widens out in the shape of a fan as we go upward, and it now appears as though we were entering the crater of a volcano. The first thing is a "Corn Mill" (from the sound of a mill grinding corn); then follows the "Ink Mill," the "Punch Bowl," the "Boiling Alum Spring," the "Devil's Arm-Chair," the "Blarney Stone," the "Witch's Caldron." This last spring is a remarkable one, about 8 feet in diameter, and of an unknown depth; temperature is said to be about 230 degrees, and will boil an egg in two minutes. Its waters are as black as ink, and are in great commotion, boiling up so fiercely as to shoot up to a considerable height, and making a loud noise. The waters of all these springs were very hot, and the ground around them was so hot that we could not stand more than a half minute in one place; for it actually burned our boots and shoes, and we were obliged to keep moving from one stone to another to prevent our feet from being burned ; and all this great heat came up through the ground on the hill-side. Near the Witches' Caldron, is the Intermittent Scalding Spring, which sometimes projects jets of hot water to a height of many feet. Next is the Stamp Mill, named from its sound. Then we reach the Steamboat Geyser, upon the shelving rock or bank, where the steam comes rushing out from an opening as large as a barrel, and shooting upward to a great height, making a loud noise, exactly resembling the loudest blowing off of a steamboat.

The next point of interest is a rock nearly 100 feet high, and on which is a flag-staff, with the American flag floating from it. This is called the "Devil's Pulpit," and it really seems out of place to have the good old star-spangled banner associated with such a name and place. We ascend laboriously to the commanding position which this place affords us. We are now on an elevated point overlooking the whole cañon, and such a sight!—looking down at the clouds, columns and jets of steam, through which we have groped our way upward to this place—and once we came near falling heavily and scalding our hands in the seething waters. The scene beggars description. We are perspiring freely from every pore, having passed over the heated and encrusted rocks, in which steps have been cut, and through blinding and stifling vapor, we feel we are about to melt, as the rocks beneath us appear to be doing, with fervent heat; the odor of brimstone has penetrated our very bones.

We have thus far merely given the names of things in this route, but the phenomenal display is wonderful. As we passed upward, the rocks beneath us, and the sloping banks on either side of us, seemed honey-combed, and the steam rushing out of a thousand openings, some small, others larger, then an immense body. The sounds were terrible and confusing, hissing, blowing, puffing, whistling, pounding, stamping, churning, grinding, till it seemed as if we were passing through a "World's Exhibition" of all its steam machinery at one place.

The rocks all the way up from the bottom of the cañon are coated with crystalizations of salt, sulphur, iron, alum, borax, magnesia, Epsom salts, ammonia, nitre, and most of the substances known in chemistry. Their color is of all shades of red, blue, yellow, orange, and green ; the color of the water is from that of the most transparent crystal to that of the blackest ink, and their tastes are indescribable.

We descended from the pulpit, and passed a few yards eastward, over the spur of the hill, and rested a few minutes in the shade of the Temperance Spring, a beautiful stream of cold water gushing out from under a cluster of large trees. This water is refreshing and invigorating, after our seething experience through the devil's dominions. In passing over the hill, our guide called our attention to the ground over which we were passing. It was the crater of another volcano. Never having seen one, except in pictures, it caused not a little surprise to our party. In passing over, I took my cane and pressed it down in the soft clayish mud-like soil about one and a half feet. On pulling out the cane, a smell of brimstone and steam came out of the hole made by it. I looked at my comrades, and made the remark that there could be no doubt that we were in the devil's dominions, and I, for one, was going to get up and get ; as I started, the others followed my example, and although there was no chance of our going down into the volcano, we all felt better when we stood on safer ground. We then passed to another spring of cold water, and found natural seats facing "Lover's Retreat," down a gorge into which a disappointed lover might leap were he so inclined. We took a seat and rested ourselves, preparatory to going into a gorge on the other side of the mountains. I should have mentioned that all around the crater there are rocks calcined by heat to an ash-colored powder, and small fragments of stone. After taking a good rest, we started down the steep declivity, and we soon came to the great "Indian Sweating Bath," where the Indians bring their

sick to be cured, by steaming powers. There is a force
and volume of steam rushing from a great opening in
the side of the mountain, among the rocks, sufficient to
propel one of our largest China ships. Further on we
find the "Tea-kettle," where the hot steam comes out
with great force, and an iron whistle has been placed,
and it gives a shrill and deafening sound near by, and
can be distinctly heard at the hotel one half mile away.

Descending the bank some distance, we come to some
rustic seats, placed under a magnificent clump of trees.
It is a delightful spot in which to rest, write, or study.
We sat down and took a good rest, and then started on
our homeward journey. Climbing over rocks, precipices and other impediments, we at last reached our hotel,
highly delighted with our afternoon visit to the Geysers.
After spending the time in rambling over the mountains,
catching a deer, fishing in the stream, we spent the evening in singing, Mrs. Gregory taking the lead, as she
generally does in that line, being a splendid singer, which
you will believe when you hear her sing some of her favorite trills. She was accompanied by other singers
boarding at the hotel, and the time was spent most agree-
ably.

After remaining almost three days longer, we were
ready to start on our journey once more ; so at 8 A. M.,
next morning, we took one of Foss' four-horse stages,
young Foss driving. He handled the lines well. He is
the son of old Foss, the world-renowned driver of San
Francisco. We were in the company of this young
man until 10 A. M., when we arrived at Pine Flats,
and here we were met by old Foss himself, with a
team of six horses. His name is Clarke Foss—as I said
before, the best driver in the Western world. Stage
driving, in this country, is an institution to be studied,
to be understood ; and the driver of a stage is the same
as an engineer of a railroad train, and, in the wild driving, though never meeting with an accident, they oftentimes become endeared to mankind ; and Clarke Foss, our

hero, stands foremost among these at the present time, and his name will be handed down in the early history of California. Seating ourselves under his care for a ride of 18 miles, let us draw his picture. He was born among the granite hills of New Hampshire, is now 53 years old, whiskers frosted with grey, eyes like the eagle, heart like a child's, voice like a commander of forces, motion quick as thought, over six feet high, weighs 240 pounds, hair black, the most perfect physique and symmetry of a man.

Away we go, with the fleetness of the wind ; the whole distance to Calestoga, where we take the cars, is 26 miles. This road twists and winds around rapidly, like an inexplicable maze, coursing along the very edge of awful chasms for seven miles, when we enter the plains of "Knight's Valley." To afford the reader a correct idea of this mountain road, over which we have just traveled, we will mention that we found 275 deep curves, and many of them so short that the leaders of our horses are out of sight on one side of projecting rocks while the stage is on the other side ; so nearly does this driver notice the motion of his carriage, that the hubs would seem to crush a fly from the rocks on one side and a mosquito from the bark of a tree on the other, always, as yet, missing the rocks on one side and never striking the tree on the other. It is most exciting to see this great man sitting in his seat holding firmly the reins of six horses in his left hand, and the whip, with its long lash, in his right hand, giving it a twirl and a crack which echoes among the rocky cliffs like the report of a pistol. The horses are trained by him ; they know his voice, and touch of rein, and crack of whip, and they obey. We say to every one who can do so, before the locomotive supplants the stage coach in California as it does in the East, or before he shall have been gathered to his fathers, to be sure to enjoy a ride over the mountains with Foss, the greatest six-horse driver in existence. And thus we go up and down until we arrive at Fossville House, the hotel of

jehu ; and this is a spot not often found in the West—
everything clean and nice, the dwelling, the stables,
horses, hens, pigs, the fruit trees, shrubs and flowers,
and the enormous oak, over seven feet in diameter, in his
front yard, looked thrifty, perfect and neat ; and here
we had one of the best dinners we had since leaving our
homes in the East. Having changed horses, we mount
again, and the road being here in good condition and
nearly level, this monarch of the lash shows us what he
and his horses can do. We start on a fast trot. At a
loud command there is a gallop--with a shout and crack
of the whip, a run. A grey squirrel was leisurely crossing the road some ways ahead ; hearing a noise, he stopped, and, seeing it was Foss, he started again just in
time to save his brush. At a word, in hardly audible
tones from the driver, the horses slow down to a gentle
trot. Away ahead, we see peeping over the trees the
domes and roofs of Calistoga. Starting again into a
gallop, then a run, with a cloud of dust reaching far
out behind us, like the tail of a comet, we enter the town,
and turning a curve full in front of the Railroad Depot,
we get out, and shaking off the dust, look back to see
where we came from away off upon the mountain ;
and in a short time we are down in the valley and
ready to take our seats in the cars for San Francisco
again, after visiting one of the great wonders of the
world.

I wish to say, when we were at Fossvile Hotel, some
of us passengers concluded to go to the petrified forest
of California, which we found was in the mountains, at
right angles with our destination, some 14 miles. We
had only two hours to do the whole trip in and get to
Calistoga in time for the cars. Foss said he could do
it, provided we could stand the journey. We answered
we would take the chances, and he hitched up another
team, of four horses this time, and off we went. The
road was splendid, but very hilly ; but Foss drove himself. And such a trip I never had before in all my life.

The horses (mustangs they were), and little ponies at that, fairly flew, never stopped until we arrived at the trees. Stayed there long enough to see one of the wonders of the West, got some specimens of the wood, and started on the return trip again. Much I could say about this remarkable trip, but as we are getting in a hurry to see the end of it, I will refrain, but will say that Foss landed us in time for the train; he said he had never yet missed doing so, although he had killed many horses in his drives.

And now, after a number of days, I find myself at the Palace Hotel, rested and ready for another trip; but remembering that this was Grand Encampment day in San Francisco, I decided to attend, and did so, and was introduced by P. G. R. Porter, was received in the usual form, and took a seat among the Patriarchs.

May the 5th. I spent this day also at the Grand Encampment, and, while there, P. G. M. Barnes and his friend Alexander came in, and we had a good time all day.

LECTURE NO. 5.

On May 7th I attended Bay City Lodge, of San Francisco, and I noticed the odes they used differed from ours, in that they were encased with tin to prevent them from wearing out so fast.

There are in San Francisco 22 Lodges, having a contingent fund of over 600,000 dollars.

Rich Lodges in San Francisco.—Grand Secretary Lyon, of California, sent me the statistical table of the 22 Lodges of San Francisco, taken from their Annual Reports for the year ending December 31st, 1876. Number of members in the city 5,289, of which 617 are P. G's, 4,104 S. D. members, 376 initiatory, and the rest divided among the different degrees ; Yerba-Buena, No. 15, has 590 members and $109,898.34 assets ; Bay City, No. 71, 241 members, and $81,293.73 ; Templar, No. 17, 490 members and $75,630.44 ; California, No. 1, 316 members, and $66,466.60 ; Harmony, No. 13, 287 members, and $58,558.47 ; Magnolia, No. 29, 285 members, and $36,769.27 ; San Francisco, No. 3, 274 members, and $31,279.83 ; Parker, No. 124, 270 members, and $27,876.-57 ; Abou Ben Adhem, No. 112, Germania, No. 116, Concordia, No. 122, and Apollo, No. 123, have each nearly 300 members, and assets of over $24,000 each. The others range about 150 members, and from $4,000 to $10,000 each. The total assets of the City Lodges, 22 in number, are $643,406.52, and, as is well known, this great amount has not been accumulated by failing to pay out to aid the distressed—by no means—for during the year $66,144.87 have been paid out for relief and charity, an average of over $3,000 per Lodge. No. 15 paid out for relief $8,043.-30 ; No. 17, $8,450.62 ; No. 13, $6,950, &c., &c., &c.

These figures are wonderful, and illustrate practical Odd Fellowship in a manner far beyond the power of oratory or argument. Our brethren of the Golden State deserve this prosperity, and may this condition of affairs be but the index of their future.

After Bay City Lodge closed, I crossed the hall into another Lodge, and there I found Brothers Barnes and Alexander singing their songs and playing, and telling their stories, which kept the Lodge in a continual roar of laughter. These two men make a good team, for both can tell a good story or sing a good song.

Tuesday, May 8th, I visited the Grand Lodge. I was introduced by D. G. M. Dann, and I was received very cordially by the brethren and invited to take a seat with them, which I did, and spent a very pleasant day. In the evening I went to Mechanics' Institute, in company with my family, and spent an evening with the Order of Ancient Odd Fellows ; P. G. R. Porter presided. Some 5,000 persons were in attendance, and the full programme was carried out, including speaking, music and singing, from the two indefatigable Odd Fellows Barnes and Alexander, who acquitted themselves to the satisfaction of all present.

May 9th. Spent this day at the Grand Lodge. Over 600 members in attendance, and they seemed to be a happy, joyous lot of men, met for the purpose of doing good in our Order. Some two hundred Past Grands took the Past Grands degree the first day. I noticed that when a brother was introduced from the East (which occurred quite often), a number of brothers would leave their seats and scrape an acquaintance with him. On inquiry, I learned that they all hailed from the same section of the country East, and felt it their duty to visit the brothers from the section of their homes, and often from their own Lodges, when at home in the East, as they call it.

The Grand Master "Tilden," of the State of California, has instituted 14 new Lodges during the year, and dedicated several new Lodge-rooms throughout the State. His report was a very distinct and cleverly written document, and was received by the members present with much satisfaction.

In the afternoon, at 4 P. M., we all started for Yosemite Valley, and arrived at Merced at 10:45 P. M. Remained there all night, and in the morning, May 11th, we took the early stage for Mariposa Village. We had five horses in our team, and we skimmed it over the dusty plains for many miles until our arrival, at 6½ P. M., and remained over night. We went through more dust on that day than in all our lives before ; forty-four miles by stage, over the dusty plains, was an event that we shall remember while life lasts. As I said before, we stopped at Mariposa over night, and after a good night's rest, we were ready to start on our dusty trip again. This country needs rain very much, it has not rained here, of any account, for the last fifteen months, and everything that grows has to be irrigated from streams running from the mountains.

We resumed our journey the next day, and traveled over hill and mountain, into dell and valley, and then up on the mountain again, and over the roughest roads I ever saw. We passed through the largest pine, blossom, cedar, oak and other kinds of woods, going over the mountains, that I ever saw in my life, yet in this country they are called common sized trees. Most beautiful sights we saw on arriving at the summit of mountains, over 6,000 feet high—we could see over 100 miles to the westward ; and after passing through and down a beautiful grove of large trees, we came in sight of Big Tree Station, where we remained over Sunday. The hotel is in the woods, alongside of the north fork of the Merced River that runs through Yosemite Valley. We found this a splendid spot to stop over Sunday. We have trout at each meal, caught from the mountain streams in this neighborhood. " Mine host" is trying to make it pleasant for us, and we have all that can be desired of a hotel in the woods ;

his name is Washburne, one of the owners of the stage line that runs to the Valley.

Sunday, May 13th. This day of rest is not thought much of here in the woods, and the people are far from any churches, schools, or religious training, and the only thing they seem to care about is how to make money off the traveler. Work of all kinds is carried on the same as other days of the week. One would think that the people here, situated as they are in the midst of God's beauties, in the very mountains on every side, would be inclined to religious thought and action, but they very soon forget about God and his works, and only strive hard for the "'mighty dollar."

During the day it tried to rain, but it failed, and now it has cleared off, and our party are trying to amuse themselves the best way that they can. Just now three men had a race. As they were running down the lane a big dog ran after them and tripped up one of them, and over he went, rolling in the dust; the dog made the best time, and we all had a good laugh.

May 14th, at 8 A. M., our party started for the big trees in Mariposa Grove, about six miles from our hotel. We were obliged to go on horseback, as they had no other mode of conveyance; no wagon road has ever been cut through the mountains to these trees, nothing but a trail to follow after, and so we started—two guides, one ahead, and the other in the rear of our party, which consists of eight travelers, a boy, two guides, making a total of eleven persons on horseback, in Indian file, as there was not room enough for two horses to walk abreast.

Some of our party had never been on horseback before, but the guides took good care of us, and after some practicing in the yard at the hotel, we all took the trail for the big trees. Now we passed through dense forests of very large trees, so they appeared to us, but they turned out only pigmies to what we saw during the day; in these same woods are also found wild animals of various kinds, such as the bear, wild-cat, deer, &c.

You must know our minds were mostly how to keep on our mustangs, or from falling down some deep declivity, and also to keep from being overhauled by some monster of the forest; and then keep in mind that riding on horseback in such a place as this—all these things put together—I tell you, we had our hands and minds full that day. It took us until eleven o'clock to get to the big trees. And such a sight; but I must not anticipate. The first thing in order was to have our lunch—the guides brought that with them—and in a short time we were regaling ourselves and preparing for the work before us. We are now 7.640 feet high, well up in the mountains, and no mistake.

Our guides give us the proper information as to these trees. There are some 700 of them in this place. There are a number of groups of large trees in California, but those in Mariposa Grove are among the largest. The largest tree is called the "Grizzly Giant;" the next one is called Lafayette; then comes the Twin Sisters, which is one tree, but which, 50 feet from the ground, separates into two branches and runs up about 200 feet further. The next was the Keystone. This tree was burned out by the Indians many years ago, and the bottom of the tree was hollow; but enough was left on the outside to hold the tree up, and the space inside was all hollow. There was eleven of us on horseback, and we all drove into this hollow place, and after getting in there was room enough left on the other side of this tree for half-a-dozen horses more, with their drivers. The next tree was blown down, and called Andy Johnson, and we walked upon its side over 250 feet as it lay there; another tree also was down, and hollow, and all of us being on horseback, the guides took the lead, and we followed them through the tree. Now this seems to you a big story, but when you take into consideration that these trees are thirty odd feet through in diameter, a hole 20 feet wide would leave 10 feet of wood and bark on either side of us, and of course, 20 feet would leave more room than was necessary for us to pass through.

After going through the foregoing tree, we all alighted
from our horses and passed up a ladder on top of the tree
which was laying on its side, and we had a dance right
on the side of the tree. The soft bark was two feet thick,
though of course, it made a nice soft spot for us to
dance on. We next come to a tall stump of a tree, about
30 feet high, all burned out inside, so we could look
through the top above. This stump is called "Pluto's
Chimney." We all passed into the hollow of this stump,
took a look upwards through the chimney, and turned
around and drove out the same way we came in. Many
of these trees are named after prominent men, and a mar-
ble slab is nailed to each tree with the name engraved
thereon. I measured some eight or nine of these trees
with some cord, and I found that the largest tree was
over 300 feet high, and 80 feet tall before you come to a
limb, and the first limb is 18 feet in thickness.

It costs a New Yorker as much to see the big trees in
California as it does to see Mont Blanc or St. Peter's.
The shortest route from San Francisco is by Merced, 139
miles eastward, thence by Washburn & Bruce's six-horse
stages, seventy-two miles up through Fremont's old
Mariposa ranch, and over the snow-capped Sierras to Big
Tree Station.

Then a mule trail of seven miles up another jagged side of the Sierras, and we stand in the great
Mariposa Grove, about 6,000 feet above the level of the
sea. This grove contains about 700 mammoth trees,
measuring from 15 to 32 feet in diameter, and from 150 to
225 feet in height. The car and stage fare from San
Francisco to the big Mariposa trees and back is $45, but
it takes about $100 to pay all expenses. But, as with
Niagara and the Pyramids, you feel amply compensated,
even if you have paid $100 for a single look. How large
are these trees? Before me now is the "Grizzly Giant."
It measures 93 feet in circumference and 31 feet in diameter. Sixty-four feet from the ground shoots out the first
limb, which is 18 feet in diameter. Its very limbs

are as large as the large forest trees that surround it. The Grizzly Giant stands among trees as a man thirty feet high would stand among men. To illustrate : Suppose in the midst of the Senate Chamber should stand up Roscoe Conkling, 30 feet high ; suppose from his right shoulder should hang Blaine, and from his left Morton, and on them should stick Sam Cox and Fernando Wood as fingers, with Ben Butler and the warlike Watterson as thumbs ; suppose Dudley Field were doubled into a nose, and Abram Hewitt and Don Cameron were twisted into ears, and Minister Evarts, the everlasting talker, mounted as a tongue ; then suppose Sam Bowles and Halstead, and Bob Ingersol and Stewart L. Woodford, were pounded up for that man's brains ; then suppose, when the giant stood up, his head should raise the Senate roof and stand along-side the dome of the Capitol, and reach out Sam Cox and Fernando Wood fingers and shake hands with the colossal statue of Liberty. If you should see that in Washington, you would have some idea how the Grizzly Giant here in the Sierras looks down on the oaks and pines, which grow like weeds at his feet—

> The giant trees, in silent majesty,
> Like pillars stand 'neath heaven's mighty dome ;
> 'Twould seem that, perched upon their topmost branch,
> With outstretched finger, man might touch the stars.

It was estimated by a lumber merchant to-day that one of the big trees, "The Mother of the Forest," contains 537,000 feet of lumber. This, at $40 per thousand, would be worth $21,480. This tree is 320 feet high and 137 feet to the first limb. The bark is twelve inches thick, and the tree is 86 feet in circumference at the base, and 43 feet in circumference 70 feet from the base.

In the Calaveras Grove five men worked twenty-two days boring a tree down with pump augurs. After boring the tree until every fiber was severed, it still stood upright. To fell it two days were spent with ropes and wedges driven in with the butts of trees. Finally the grand old monarch fell, after standing the blasts of 3,000 years. Then they smoothed off the stump, and on the Fourth of July thirty-two persons danced on it. Our party, consisting of about fifteen, chased around on this stump, but to me it was with a painful feeling. It was like dancing around the tomb of the dead Napoleon. Yes, like dancing on the fallen monument to a dead god. This stump is 28 feet across—three feet wider than a New York building lot—and sound to the center. It would take sixty-four yards of carpet to cover it. This tree was 302 feet high,—higher than the dome of the Capitol or than Trinity steeple.

The Father of the Forest is another grand old fallen monarch. This tree fell many years ago. It was 375 feet high and 28 feet thick. It being hollow we rode our horses into its hollow trunk 82 feet. The height of the horseback entrance is 10 feet; the diameter of the trunk 150 feet from the roots is 10 feet 4 inches.

In the Mariposa Grove we came to a large hollow tree called the Keystone. Eight of us rode our horses through it at one time. It had been burnt out, and lived in by the Indians, but still looked fresh and vigorous at the top.

In the South Park Grove our party all disappeared in a big tree called the "Grand Hotel," the hollow trunk of which will hold forty persons. Near by is Noah's Ark, now fallen, but which measures 90 feet in circumference, and 320 feet in length, and just beyond is an unnamed tree, in the hollow of which 16 horses can stand.

How many of these big trees are there?

There are in California, within 25 miles of the Yosemite Valley, five groves of these big trees. The Calaveras Grove, north of the Yosemite, contains 94 trees; the South Park Grove, six miles nearer the Yosemite, contains 1,380 trees, from 10 to 90 feet in circumference. The Tuolumne Grove contains 30 trees, and the Mariposa 700, making the total number of big trees (*Sequoia gigantea*) in existence in the world 2,214.

Will the number of big trees increase?

There is no reason why they should not, although I find only a few young ones growing. The fires run through the woods every year, and this undoubtedly kills the little trees. The seed from the big trees can be easily gathered. Indeed, I gathered perhaps 500 seeds and sent them to friends in different parts of the country.

To what species does the big tree belong?

No similar tree is found elsewhere. It more closely resembles the common American cedar, such as grows in the swamps between Syracuse and Utica, than any other tree. In the same soil, a sandy loam, grow in numberless millions, gigantic pines, yellow and white. Many of them are 7 feet in diameter and 60 feet to a limb. The common balsam or fir, such as grows from 4 to 30 inches in diameter in New York, also grow here 6 and 7 feet in diameter and 225 feet high, and the hop-pole cedar, which never gets beyond 30 inches in diameter in New York, here grows to 3 feet in diameter, with a ragged bark, which one can hardly distinguish from the *Sequoia gigantea.* The red wood trees which grow down on the California coast to 10 feet in diameter, also closely resemble the big trees.

How old are these trees?

I counted the concentric rings on the stump of a big tree—and all botanists agree that each ring represents a year's growth—and they numbered 3,840, so the tree was 3,840 years old. We find many big trees, from 1,500 to 4,000 years old.

The altitude of the big trees makes them grow in almost perpetual snow. On the 15th of May, when we could see them cradling their wheat in the San Joaquin Valley, the frosty winds howled through the big trees, the frozen sleet frosted the limbs of the big trees, and we defiled our horses down the jagged mountain side toward the Yosemite in a foot of snow. There is so much to tell you about these wonderful monarchs of the forest that I hardly know where to stop ; but I have much yet to in-form you of, and so we will leave these trees and start for the Big Tree Station, where we arrive at 5 P. M., very tired and lame, riding on horseback, but feeling well pleased with the day's sight-seeing.

May 15th. This day our little party started a six-horse coach for the Yosemite Valley, only 24 miles from here. The night of the 14th it had rained and snowed, and on the next morning we found the hills covered with snow. One thing certain, we were not to be troubled with dust this day, but we found it very cold, wet and raw, and we were obliged to put on extra wraps. At one time we were over 8,000 feet high. We passed through immense forests of pine, cedar, and other kinds of trees, and over high mountains and down into deep dells, and at one time four deer crossed our path. Frank tried to get a crack at them with his 34 shooting iron, but like other hunters that we wot of, when he was ready to shoot the game was out of range, for which I was very glad.

After a tedious ride, we at last came in sight of the wonderful valley at " Inspiration Point."

We were going down a steep declivity, when suddenly there arose a shout from our little party. Every ear was open, and every eye was too—and such a shout as we gave, I knew that the valley had revealed itself to our vision. We got out, and bent our steps to a prominent point, and I crawled upon the overhanging rocks, over 4,000 feet, right straight down to the bottom of the valley. In all my life, let it lead me where it will, I think I shall never see anything so grand, so awful, so sublime, so beautiful!—beautiful with beauty, not of this earth, as the vision of this valley seen by us from " Inspiration Point" that day.

It is now over nine months since we were there, and yet not a day passes over my head but that I think of it, and I could have remained there until now. My opinion is that I can travel over every spot on this globe, but will never see anything that can be compared to it. I brought the picture of it with me, and I have only to shut my eyes and I see it as I saw it then, in that hour of hours ; I think I shall see nothing else so sublime and beautiful till, happily, I shall stand within the gates of the heavenly city above. But we are some distance yet from our hotel. However enchanting this spot is, we must not linger here too long ; but as the driver calls us away, then away we go, take our seats, and off we go down a deep declivity into the valley below. Many times since my return home have I thought of my position on the end of that high rock at Inspiration Point, and I have as often shut my eyes, and in imagination looked again out from that point.

Many persons have tried to tell their neighbors just how they felt while standing at Inspiration Point the first time, and different expressions have been used in giving vent to their thoughts. As for me, I felt lost in wonder, love and praise.

The remarks of our little party were curious. The words were not many. Some said next to nothing, but kept drinking in the beauties and wonders before them ; others were exclaiming oh ! continually, and as we proceeded down the very steep road, at times, a general unanimous " Oh ! oh !" and " look there," "aint that nice ?" and other words of praise coming from all of us, as the sight of some peculiar rock or sheet of water would first strike our attention. On the opposite side of where we were going down is a high rock, 3,300 feet high, called the " Le Capitain." This rock is actually perpendicular in front. It commands our attention until we get down into the valley, when our attention was called to a stream of water (on our right, opposite to " Le Capitain") coming over the rocks, and appeared as if we were right under it. It is called the Bridal Veil Falls, 950 feet high. The stream is not very large, and when the wind blows against this fall the water is blown in every direction, and is very misty, and resembles a bridal veil hanging from a bride's forehead.

You, who have been to Niagara Falls, recollect how

very high it looks when you are down near the bottom of
the Falls. Well, just compare the Bridal Veil Falls
with those at Niagara—one 190 feet high, and the other
950 feet, five times greater. But it is near 5 P. M., and
we are all complaining of being very hungry, so we hurry
up, and after passing through pretty near the whole
length of the valley, we stop at our hotel, called the
"Yosemite Falls Hotel," kept by Mr. John K. Barnard.
This hotel is built (at least one end of it is) over a river
called the Merced. A neat tidy hotel it is.

After resting a while, I started with my family for the
Yosemite Falls, directly opposite to the hotel on the other
side of the river. We wandered up over rocks and falls
of water, crossed over on logs, and finally brought up at
the foot of the Yosemite Falls, 2,634 feet high, fourteen
times as high as Niagara. Now just imagine another
falls, just fourteen times as high as old Niagara, and by
comparing the two, you will fix in your mind how high
the Yosemite Falls are. After viewing this wonderful
sight for over an hour, we returned to our hotel, and retired early to gain strength for the morrow's work.

May 16. This was a rainy, cloudy day, and but little
sight-seeing was done by us, on account of the fog settling down upon us like a pall. In the afternoon the fog
lifted and the rain ceased, and after dinner, we took a
carriage and went to the foot of the Bridal Veil Falls,
and afterward returned home.

I noticed at our hotel there was a fine tree growing
right up through the roof, in the parlor. This tree is
over 9 feet in diameter and over 30 feet around—quite an
ornament for a lady's parlor, I hear you say. Well that
is so, and it is one of the sights of the valley, and a great
curiosity it is to sight-seers.

After the fatigue and excitement of the day's ride, and
the novel circumstances of the past few days, it is natural to suppose that with a comfortable bed will come refreshing sleep ; yet experience proves the contrary, for it
seems a luxury to lie awake listening to the sparkling,

washing, roaring, swaying, hissing, seething, sound of the great Yosemite Falls just opposite to our hotel, or, passing quietly out of our resting place, look up between the lofty pines or spreading oaks to the giant cliffs, that tower up with such majesty of form and boldness of outline against the vast ethereal vault of heaven, or watch in the moonlight the ever-changing shapes and shadows of the water, as it lays on the cloud-draped summit of the mountains, and falls in gusty torrents on the unyielding granite, to be dashed to infinity of atoms; then we return to our welcome couch, and dream of some genius of immense proportions extending over us his protecting arms, and of his admonishing the water-fall to modulate the music of its voice that we may sleep and be refreshed.

May 17. Sometime before the sun can get a good honest square look at us, deep down as we are in this awful chasm, we see him painting his rosy smiles on the ridges and shadows in the furrows of the mountains' brow, as though he took a pride in showing up to the best advantage the wrinkles time had made upon it; but all of us feel too fatigued to fully enjoy the thrilling grandeur and beauty that surrounds us, and so we sleep on, taking our rest, until we are awakened by the ringing of the breakfast bell. We jump up, dress ourselves very quickly, and are down at our breakfast in a very short time. After breakfast we consult our guides, and a plan for the day is mapped out.

We take another trip to the Yosemite Falls. High boulders and large masses of sharp angular rocks are scattered here and there, forming the uneven sides of an immense and apparently over-boiling caldron, around and in the interstices of which numerous dwarf ferns, weeds, grasses and flowers are ever growing. It is beyond the power of language to describe the awe-inspiring majesty of the darkly frowning and overhanging mountain walls of solid granite that here hem us in on every side, as though they would threaten us with instantaneous destruction, if not total annihilation, did we attempt for a moment to deny their power. If man ever feels his utter insignificance at any time, it is when looking upon such a scene of appalling grandeur as the one here presented.

After lingering here for some time, with inexpressible feelings of astonishment and delight, gratified and intensified by veneration, we take a long and reluctant last gaze upward, convinced that we shall never look upon its like again, we make our way back as best we can to our hotel, feeling as if we had lost a friend.

Our guide announces that the coach is waiting to take us to Mirror Lake. Much of the beauty of this lake consists in its reflection of its glorious surroundings, mountains 4,000 to 5,000 feet high all around the lake. It is desirable to start for the lake at an early hour; sometimes the unbroken calm of its glassy bosom is not disturbed before noon, at other times the breeze has broken it up by 10 o'clock, but generally the mirror is perfect until nearly noon. The distance from the hotel to the lake is only three miles.

On arriving at the lake we find it in perfect order ; and oh——h, such a sight!—man never saw anywhere else anything like it. It is one of the wonders of the valley, surrounded as it is on all sides by very high mountains, the reflections of which can be seen so plainly in the water—each tree, branch, shrub, twig and leaf, can be seen reflected so plainly.

After remaining at the lake long enough to see all the sights connected with the mirror-lake, we retraced our steps back to the hotel again. But let me describe this beautiful sheet of crystal water of almost two acres in extent, in which numerous schools of speckled trout may be seen gaily disporting themselves ; it would be unworthy of notice but for the picturesque grandeur of its surroundings. On the north and west sides lie immense rocks that have become detached from the tops of the mountains above. Among these grow a large variety of trees and shrubs, many of which stand on and over the margin of the lake, and are reflected on its mirror-like bosom. To the

northwest opens a vast gorge or cañon, down which impe-
tuously rush the waters of the north fork of the Merced
River, which runs into and supplies the lake. On the
south-east stands the majestic Mount Lis-sa-ak, or the
South Dome, as it is most generally called, 6,000 feet
high above the valley. Almost half of this immense
mass of solid rock, as it appears to us, either from some
convulsion of nature, or time's effacing fingers, has fallen
over, by which most probably the dam of Mirror Lake
was first formed ; yet, proudly and defiantly erect, this
great mass of rocks still holds its noble head, and is not
only the highest of all those around, but is the greatest
attraction of the valley.

We are back at our hotel again, and are preparing ourselves to go on horseback to the Vernal and the Nevada
Falls ; but, before we start, I wish to introduce you to a
great rock, back of our hotel, called the Sentinel Rock,
4,000 feet high, a lofty and solitary peak by itself, upon
which the watch fires of the Indians have often been
lighted to give warning of approaching danger, and
which can be seen from all the principal points within
and around the valley.

It is now 10 A. M. The guide gives the word to advance, and as we are now all on horseback, the guide is
ahead, and we follow on after. Oh, I wish you could
have seen us as we passed up through the valley in Indian file, keeping close to the guide, for you could lose
the trail very easily alone, and so we all make love to our
guide--and I notice our ladies were very anxious to make
his acquaintance—and it was guide here and guide there ;
and this was kept up most of the time as we were
going up through the valley to the falls just mentioned. On our right is a high wall of granite, nearly
perpendicular, 4,000 feet high, called the Glacier Point,
down which several ribbon-like streams of water are leap-
ing ; here and there, from the sides of this great mountain, a single tree or shrub is standing alone. On our left
stands the Royal Arches, 2,000 feet high, Washington's

Tower, say 5,000 feet high above the valley, then the North Dome and South Dome, and other objects to be observed, numerous majestic trees overshadowing the way ; flowers of many kinds are abundant, such as the yellow and purple evening primrose, the larkspur, and also a very pretty pink, called the everlasting ; but, to give a complete list of all the roses and flowers, would complete a volume.

About two miles above our hotel we arrive at and continue on the southern bank of the Merced River, beneath a bower of trees and shrubs, over the roughest portion of the trail. Formerly visitors used to tie their horses here, and make the ascent on foot ; but some recent improvements now induce visitors to ride nearly up to the Vernal Falls. On our left the river forms a foaming cataract to the very foot of the falls, and the thundering boom of its waters rises at times above the sound of human voices. Upward and onward we climbed, and after passing a bold point, called the Register-Rock, we obtain suddenly the first sight of Vernal Falls ; the Indian name is Li-roy-ock, meaning a shower of sparkling crystals. We keep on climbing onward and upward, and at times very steep places, until we are at Snow's Hotel, under the Cap-of-Liberty mountain, a tremendous rock ;—it stands boldly out at the north side of Nevada Falls. This great rock is nearly 7,000 feet high.

After dismounting we proceeded to the hotel, kept by a Mrs. Snow, formerly from Vermont; this lady sets a splendid table for her visitors ; but she is in a state of intoxication pretty much all the while, and in that state she tried to make it pleasant for us ; her dough-nuts and pumpkin pies are spoken of as the very best ever made by a Vermonter, and while we praise her cooking and the good dough-nuts, and the splendid table she sets, we must enter our protest against her trying to ape drunken men's actions. Well, after our lunch, we strolled around seeing the sights presented to our view from every side. This hotel is situated between the Nevada and the Vernal

Falls. On our left, directly in front of the hotel, is Nevada Falls, 700 feet high, and right directly in the rear of this hotel is the Vernal, some 400 feet high—the two falls—the waters falling some 1,100 feet ; and on our immediate left is the Cap of Liberty, a great mass of rock or mountain, where man seldom, if ever, has placed his foot. And, to our right, another mountain, still higher, looming up into the air. Now, I think, I have given you a pretty clear idea of our position ; and after a good rest, the guide took the horses down the way we came up, into the bottom of the mountain valley, and we started to follow the river down the steep and precipitous way winding down to the bottom of the cañon, where we would find the guide and horses waiting for us. Well, we started down one of the most hazardous and dangerous trails ever traveled by woman, and I might say also by man. On arriving at the top of the lower fall—the Vernal—there we were some 400 feet above the bottom of it. How to get down we did not know ; but on looking around under a high rock we spied a path leading to a pair of stairs, very steep, almost perpendicular, down which we picked our way, placing our feet firmly in the right position, we, as it were, felt our way down those difficult stairs. The men of our company had but little trouble, but the ladies were not so well blessed, for their skirts were in the way continually ; but they were dressed pretty much after the Bloomer costume, and, for a woman, each one did first rate; and in the course of an hour or so we finally landed safe and sound-at the foot of the falls, down where we found the guide with our horses waiting for us. So far as myself was concerned, I had not a dry thread on me. I had a short rope with me— my wife had hold of one end, while I was at the other ; we manged to get down very well, although I came to the conclusion that the rope saved our lives more than once. We had a good rest, and then mounted our beasts and started for our homes, very tired, but very thankful for the sight-seeing and for our safe arrival at our hotel, for it did appear as if some of us would lose our lives before we should get back again.

May 18th. This day six of us went to Glacier Point; and this trip was done on horseback also. You see our little party is still less than yesterday ; but our sight-seeing was too much yesterday, and so to-day they are at the hotel viewing the sights, while we are trying to go up a perpendicular rock, on a trail cut right into the side of the rock ; and as we commenced to ascend and look around, we noticed two or three other companies of men and women winding up this terribly steep ascent. After a tedious ride, we at last come to a place where we dismount and take a rest, and as we are the first up at Union Point, we watch the other travelers coming up, and try to make out who they all are. The first party is Chaplain McCabe and his friends ; we have a good shake of hands with the chaplain, and we are introduced to his friends. Pretty soon another announcement is made, Frank Leslie and his friends arrive at Union Point. The horses are all taken care of by the guides, and a general hand-shake all around takes place among the friends thrown together at this peculiar place, of about one acre of level land and rock. On counting the entire number, we find 30 horses waiting for the guests to mount, and, after being rested, we all started on the final route for Glacier Point. As we were the first to arrive at Union Point, we were the first to mount and start ahead. On looking back, after we all had got under weigh, the sight was splendid ! wonderful ! Thirty horses and riders groping their way up the mountain sides was a sight not often seen even here, and it left a peculiar sensation that I shall never forget. We at last arrived at Glacier Point, over 4.000 feet high, and, before looking around, we came to the conclusion of having our dinner. We found, away up here, a building put up for refreshments. We had our dinner, and then started out for sight-seeing. We started for the place where the whole valley can be seen with one sweep of the eye. Before looking down, let me call your attention to a somewhat noticeable projecting point that is seen from our hotel below, apparently extending out some three or four feet, but we find—when standing near to it to-day—to be over 30 feet beyond the wall. Some time ago a photographer stood on the end of this rock projecting out, and took a splendid view of the valley. and its surroundings.

Now let us advance to the edge of this awful precipice ; we can steady ourselves by holding on to the large rock at our side, or we can lie down on the great rock on which we stand, having some one to hold us by our feet while we slide out to its utmost edge. It may make us a little nervous perhaps, the first time, but taking all necessary precautions, we shall find it unaccompanied by any real danger ; and we shall certainly never regret that our courage was equal to the task of one good look at least into such an awful abyss. And oh ! such a sight ; man never looked on before in any other place on this globe like it, over 4,000 feet in height, straight up and down, perpendicular indeed, into the valley below. The greatest artists have invariably failed in photographing depth from a high stand-point, and we do not know of any writer being more successful than the artist. We wish for our friends, who are not here to see with their own eyes, that the coming man had arrived who could do this which has not been accomplished by any man as yet. Under these circumstances we are willing, with our commonplace eyes, to try to tell you what we saw : Large trees, over 200 feet high, sink into utter insignificance ; the little checkerboard-like spot, first noticed in Mr. Lemon's apple orchard, and contains over 500 trees 20 feet apart ; the bright speck, which throws out its silver light in that deep tree-dotted cañon, is Mirror Lake, while that South Dome overshadows every lesser wonder, and towers aloft a little on our right ; then comes the North Dome ; clouds rest on Cap of Liberty ; Mount Star-King, Yosemite Falls, and other prominent objects here visible, would have their due effect, but although at this height and position, they

differ altogether in outline, the South Dome stands king
over all; on the right of this monarch, in the deep gorge
of the river, the magnificent Nevada Fall, Diamond Flume
and Apron, Vernal Fall, and the foaming cataract of the
Nevada Fall and Merced River, all flash out their silver
light, while mountains, piled on mountains in every conceivable shape, stand grandly on every side ; and on our
left, as we look down the valley, the first high rock,
standing out very plain, and called the Sentinel Dome ;
this dome is near 4,000 feet high, and had it been scalped
by some tornado, it could have scarcely shown less vegetation, for, with the exception of one or two stunted
trees, there is scarcely a vestige of a thing living upon it.
On the side opposite to us, in the distance, are some very
high peaks of mountains of the Sierra Nevada range,
that can be seen very plainly from this stand-point. Let
me enumerate some of them—I see them now : Mount
Hoffman, 10,872 feet high ; Cathedral Peak, 11,000 feet
high ; Mount Dana, 13,227 feet high ; Mount Lyall, 12,270
Castle Peak, 12,500 feet high ; Gothic Peak, 10,850 feet
high ; Mount Star-King, 9,600 feet high ; Dome, 10,000 feet
high, and numerous other peaks are seen very high, but
I forget their names. Did time permit we might very
probably tarry here for days, as new beauties would be
opening and strange forms made manifest on every side.
But there is so much to tell you about what we saw and
witnessed here to-day, and our time is passing away so
rapidly, that you will please excuse our haste for the
rapid decline of the sun in the west reminds us of returning ; so let us not attempt the danger of going down that
awful trail in the dark, but let us start now. But I wish
to say that Frank Leslie had his photographer and
sketcher along, and all day long they were kept busy in
sketching and photographing whatever might fall in their
way ; Mrs. Gregory and my wife are sketched lying on
the rock looking over into that awful abyss ; Mrs. Gregory is represented as holding on to my wife's skirts to
keep her from falling 4,000 feet below, while they were

placed in that position. You, who take that paper, "Frank Leslie's Illustrated," will in time see the picture of our party going up the mountains on horseback, and while they were on the mountains, as I stated just now.

Well, we are down again once more into the valley. I was the only one of our party who stuck to his mustang coming down that perpendicular hill, all of the others got scared, got off, and led their horses down.

Well, here we are at our hotel once more, and more than thankful that we have escaped the seeming danger of breaking our necks. A few notes about the valley, river views, forest openings, rocky points, water-falls, heads of men and women, outlined in shadows on water-stained rocks, and right upon the vertical walls of granite, with numerous other objects to attract and interest, are all in the way to be seen through this wonderful place.

May 19th. This day all hands started for the back track again to San Francisco, and at 6 o'clock, A. M., our party, of eight persons, took one of Washburn's stages and started down the valley to go up to Inspiration Point, and, as we arrive at this place, we stop to have one more and a long and last look of Yosemite Valley. After a length of time, winding up the never-to-be-forgotten road that leads into the valley, Inspiration Point is reached.

There is a saying, that "some things can be done as well as others." In my opinion, a full description of this scene is not one of them. A passage in the good book says : "eye hath not seen, neither hath the ear heard, neither hath it entered into the heart of man to conceive, what there is laid up in heaven for those who love and serve God." Now, without wishing to detract from the interesting assertion there so graphically pictured and offered, we simply wish to apply the language to those who have the good fortune to see Yosemite Valley from this stand-point ; we hope so, as we can only give a few plain facts, and leave you to do the sublime. Remember we are standing on a precipice of 4,000 feet high, the whole valley and its surroundings are spread out before us like a map, the river below is like a ribbon of silver, seen only at intervals winding among trees, the trees themselves resembling mere shrubs ; the grand old sides and proud head of old " Le Capitaine," looms grandly upwards ; the same for the North Dome, and the clouds rest on the Sentinel Dome, with any number of others.

Just let me run over the principal objects that can be seen from Inspiration Point, just where we are now : the Ribbon, a fall of water alongside of old "Le Capitaine," 3,300 feet high ; Upper Yosemite Fall, 2,634 feet high ; Bride's Veil Fall, 950 feet high ; Three Brothers Rocks, which are three rocks, one projecting over the other, 4,000 feet high ; Three Grace's Rocks, 3,750 high ; " Le Capitain" Rock, right in front of us, 3,300 feet high ; Sentinel Rock, 3,720 feet high ; the Cathedral Rock, 2,690 feet high ; Royal Arches, a rock 1,800 feet high ; Washington Tower, 2,200 feet high ; Glacier Point, 4,000 feet high ; North Dome, 4,000 feet high ; Cap of Liberty Rock, 5,240 feet high ; South Dome, 6,000 feet high ; Vernal Falls, 400 feet high ; Lower Yosemite Fall, 600 feet high ; Nevada Falls, 700 feet high ; and the Sentinel Rock, 4,000 feet high.   There are many more objects to be seen and to be mentioned, but you will agree with me that the foregoing named places are enough to fill us with a sense of awe ! of splendor! and of inspiration!   And this is why this place is called Inspiration Point, for in five minutes after leaving here we lose the sight, and that forever, unless we return at some future time into this valley.   If the storm has been gathering, perhaps we can see it sweep down on the wings of the wind, and drape the whole landscape in clouds.   At times the whole valley is filled with them, piled layer above layer, stratum above stratum, to the very tops of the mountains.   Now Inspiration Point stands out and up at a somewhat greater altitude than most of the foregoing-mentioned objects, and the view of the distant Sierra Nevadas is more comprehensive.   The general view of both being similar, there is no necessity for any further remarks, therefore let us enjoy the scene in peaceful silence, and when we can say "enough," let us depart on our own winding-way, and then dream of what we have seen. But we cannot leave this sacred spot (to us at least) until we have given you the dimensions of it: The altitude of Yosemite is given at 4,060 feet. It is about 8 miles long, from ½ mile to 1¼ miles wide, surrounded by walls in many places perpendicular, from 3,000 to 6,000 feet high. Its general course is north-east and south-west; from one end to the other there is a fall of 50 feet; the number of acres of every kind of land is 36,111 ; the main Merced River is about 80 feet wide, and perfectly clear, and runs through the entire length of the valley ; trout, in reasonable quantities, can be seen at almost any point of the river; numerous kinds of trees and shrubs grow through it; ferns, flowers and grasses grow in almost endless quantities and varieties. The atmosphere is very temperate, bracing and healthy, both summer and winter, the thermometer seldom running above 80° in the summer, or more than 16° below freezing point in the winter—a cool breeze from the northwest in the morning, and from the northeast at night, keeps the valley in summer at a very comfortable temperature. Snow falls in winter from three to five feet in depth. The sun rises at our hotel, in the shortest day of the year, at half-past one in the afternoon and sets at half-past three, the day being only of two hours' duration in winter.

Rain and snow generally comes from the south. No communication with the outer world for about six months in the year. In winter an Indian mail-carrier takes the mail to the citizens in the valley once in three months, on foot. It is much to be regretted that the tourist should allow himself so brief a period in this wonderful valley, usually only from three to four days, when he should remain at least fourteen. After he has left its sublime solitudes, its numerous waterfalls and brooklets, its picturesque river scenes, its groups of trees and shrubs, its endless variety of wild flowers, its bold, ragged, awe-inspiring, pine-studded and snow-covered mountains, with all their ever-changing shadows and curious shapes and its health-giving charms, that would have given pleasurable occupation and grateful variety to every class and condition, both of body and mind, for months, he contrasts that he saw with that he might have seen, and becomes dissatisfied with his course in spending so much time as well as money in traveling there and riding off without seeing more than a limited portion of such remarkable scenes. Wishing all a safe and joyous return, with none but pleasant memories forever of their trip to the Yosemite, we bid each agreeable companion a reluct ant "good bye."

And now, as we leave Inspiration Point, we all jump into our coach, take a long look at old Yosemite Valley, sit down, and the driver asks the question, Are you all ready? Not one answered, for we all felt as though we were parting with our best friend, and hated to say go on, but the driver took silence for consent, and with the crack of the whip off we go up the high mountains, and in a few moments we are out of sight of Yosemite Valley, and at 12½ A. M. arrived at Big Tree Station, and at 2 P. M. we started for Mariposa and arrived there at 8 P. M.

In the afternoon, Frank shot a Jack Rabbit, and after that tried to shoot another, standing alongside of the driver on the stage. In so doing the three leading horses took fright, jumped ahead, and broke the double whiffle-tree, and there we were fifteen miles from any house, but after awhile the driver fixed it up so we could go on again. Frank did not attempt to shoot off that gun again, but from a little what I said he came to the conclusion to put the gun up and cause no more disturbance. Once more we started ahead, and on going down a steep mountain we ran foul of a rock on the side of the road, and it made everything crack, and we began to think we would be obliged to stay out all night, for it appeared as if the hind axletree was broken, but on getting out and shov-

ing the coach back we found everything all right, and so
we reseated ourselves and once more started ahead, and
after ten miles more of driving arrived at Mariposa,
thankful for our safe arrival, and the next morning, May
20th, Sunday, started for Merced, and I wish to say this
was the first time we traveled on God's day from our
first start. We timed it so that when Sunday came we
were not on the road breaking the Sabbath, and I think we
got on a little better than those who never make arrange-
ments for stopping over on Sunday ; but this Sunday we
were obliged to be out till 2 P. M., at which time we
arrived at Merced, where we had previously left our
trunks when starting for the Valley in the stage. We
remained at the hotel, our little party breaking up and
going in different directions. We took the train at 11
P. M., and went to Lower California, 500 miles down the
coast to Los Angelos. Nothing of note occurred, and we
arrived next morning. I had heard much of Lower
California, but this trip was not a very satisfactory one.
We simply traveled all day through sand, dust, and wind.
It appeared as if this was the last feather to the
camel's back in the way of dust and sand down the Sierra
Nevada Mountain Valley. It is a crooked railroad and
no mistake. On going over these mountains the conductor called our attention to a hole away up in the
mountain, right over our heads, and he said we would
have to pass through that hole. I could hardly believe
him, but I noticed the winding road right up over this
tremendous mountain, and I noticed we crossed our own
track, and after a number of windings and short cuts we
at last did pass right through the hole, called Tunnel No.
9, and there were no less than seventeen of these tunnels
to go through in ascending the mountain. The engineering on this railroad, I am told, is ahead of anything of
its kind in this country, and I believe it to be true, and
it is worth the time and expense of a man who loves
engineering to go and have a good look at this great
work of running a train up the side of a mountain many

thousand feet high. Nothing further of note transpired, and we arrived at Los Angelos in time for dinner. In the evening I visited a lodge of Odd Fellows called Augablia Lodge No. 195, and spent a very pleasant evening. P. G. M. Hill, of California, delivered an address on Odd Fellowship in General, and as he is a speaker as well as a preacher he had no difficulty in telling his story in a common sense way.

May 22d was spent in taking a ride to the Orange Grove in near vicinity. We had a very pleasant time in passing through miles of orange and fruit groves. We were well received by the owners of the ranches and gardens as we went along. We saw many kinds of fruit and plants, such as acorns, pepper trees, English walnuts, bananas, butternuts, oranges, peaches, etc., also a real tree of Lebanon, and many other kinds of trees, the names of which I do not remember. We also passed a garden of thirty-four kinds of flowers and roses, with which the owner loaded us down. We also stopped at a mission church called the San Gabriel Mission, a Spanish building over 104 years old, a Roman Catholic church. They were holding services when we arrived there.

We also called upon Col. McEwan, who owns a beautiful ranch. He has a great liking for beautiful flowers and shrubs. We were invited into his house, the walls of which are nine feet thick. It is called the Emoline House, 130 years old. Years ago, every man's house was his castle, and Spanish robbers were plenty, and the owners were obliged to defend themselves from the highwaymen. I also noticed that the well of water was made in the wall of the house, and drawn from the inside of the building. We had a splendid time with the Colonel, and then retraced our steps homeward. In the evening I attended Orange Grove Encampment No. 31, and spent a very pleasant evening.

May 23d, Mrs. Gregory and my wife went some fifty miles to see Mrs. Gregory's brother, who has a Bee

Ranch. We are to meet again in San Francisco next Sunday. Frank and myself went to Sante Maneco, about 17 miles, a seaport town on the Pacific coast, and we shipped on board the steamship Orizaba for San Francisco. It seemed natural once more to go on board a water craft, this time on the great Pacific Ocean. It made me think of my business and my home again. May 24th I was awakened by the firing of a gun at Santa Barbara. This is the Long Branch of the Pacific Coast, and a great watering place for the Western people. The climate is very mild, and the town is almost surrounded by high mountains, although right on the coast. After taking in more passengers we resumed our voyage. There were two big Sea Lions on board, as freight, in boxes, and as I went near them they showed fight and commenced to growl. They seemed dissatisfied with their position, and stuck out their heads and growled like a dog, and they tried to bite me.

We stopped at a place called Garioli, and took on 800 sheep and lambs for the San Francisco market. The manner of getting them on board is wonderful. They were put in the ship's hold in twenty minutes, by leading a lamb ahead then the whole lot would follow. On the same pier where our ship lay was a steamship called Wm. Taber, bound for Sacramento, loading with cattle for market, and the way the owners got these steers on board was curious. A gangway is built, box-like, to the vessel ; the cattle are all up in a corral ; the drivers, who are Mexicans, are on horseback ; these cattle are run down the dock as fast as they can go by the drivers and horses ; halloing, shouting, and using their long goads, they are kept in the gangway, and before they are aware of it are compelled to go on board the ship. The cattle oftentimes become crazed, and they show fight, but the herders, with their long goads, whip and frighten the animals until they give up and rush on the gangway on board the ship, many of them more dead than alive. We continued up the Pacific Coast 500 miles, until we

came in sight of the seal rocks at the Golden Gate. At
4½ P. M., we went through the gate into the harbor of
San Francisco, and at 5 P. M. we landed at the wharf
and made a bee line for the hotel, where we remained for
the next three days waiting for the lady members of our
party to come from the lower end of California. They
hove in sight on Sunday, about noon.

May the 28th, in the morning, at 8 o'clock, we all
started for home in New York. We took the palace
drawing-room provided for us, and the first stopping-
place was Sacramento, and then to Ogden, where we
changed to the Northern Pacific for Omaha.

Our company was increasing, as we went along, and
when at Ogden we became acquainted with Dr. Chase,
of Illinois, a splendid tenor singer, also Chaplain
McCabe and his friends, and altogether we had a splendid time in coming over the mountains ; singing by Mrs.
Gregory, Mr. Chase, the Doctor, Mr. Marsh and Chaplain
McCabe about all the time ; then all of us would chime in
and we had a glorious time.

When at Reno we took Mr. Frank Leslie and party on
board. They came in their own car.

May 29th. This day passed through the Humboldt
Valley again, and it snowed all day long. Although the
the weather was good, snow storms were out of order,
so it seemed to us.

We had some fun with Mrs. Leslie and her poodle-
dog this morning. At all of our eating stations Mrs.
Leslie would carry her poodle to the table with her.
While at the breakfast table at Humboldt the dog began
to bark at the Chinamen waiters with their long pig-tails
behind them. Mrs. Leslie could not keep the "little
nuisance" still, and so she picked him up and strode
down the aisle of the room to go on board her car.
Every eye was on the woman, and the dog kept barking
at the Chinamen all the way out. Mr. Leslie kept his
seat until the woman and dog had disappeared ; he
seemed to dislike the scene very much ; his actions spoke

plainer than words that he wished the Chinaman would cut the dog's tail off close behind his ears.

May 30th, arrived at Laramie plains, the highest point on the railroad, 8,242 feet high. From here we descend very fast, for we are now on the top of the Rocky Mountains, and the weather is very cold, rain and snow continually.

Arrived at Cheyenne, and our number is increased by the addition of Mr. Gregory, who meets us here.

June 1st. Arrived at Omaha, at 3:45 P. M., and here Mr. and Mrs. Gregory left us, and remained at Omaha over night, while we went on to Chicago, where we arrived at 4 P. M. the next day.

June 2d. We passed through a most beautiful country ; everything along the route looked thrifty and well kept, the country and the beautiful farms look so nice. It appears that this was the garden of beautiful farms, and rich men enjoy themselves as only wealthy farmers can. What a difference in the looks of the country. We have been running through a beautiful valley, called the '' Boyer Valley.'' We are still in the State of Iowa. We crossed the Mississippi River at Clinton at 9 A. M. and what a stream this father of waters is. We have crossed the bridge into the State of Illinois, and we find the weather very warm, more so than we had experienced since leaving Brooklyn three months previous. At 4 P.M. we arrived at Chicago, and went to the Sherman House. My wife is complaining, and is quite sick, and has been so since leaving San Francisco, and to-day she is not able to go down to her meals.

June 3d. Found my wife some better, and being Sunday, I went to the First M. E. Church, returned, took dinner, and strolled through the city to see the sights, also went to Lake Michigan, a splendid body of water. I was in Chicago in 1843, but what a change since then. In the afternoon Mr. and Mrs. Gregory arrived from Omaha, and the next day we took a carriage and drove through the city to the place where the great fire started ; also, the water-works, where they tunneled under the lake two miles so as to get pure water for the city. After dinner I called on Mr. J. Ward Ellis, one of the leading Odd Fellows of the town, and had a talk with him. He it was who received our donation for the suffering Odd Fellows of the city after the great fire, and I found, on examination, that except from San Francisco, that old Atlantic Lodge paid more money than any other Lodge in the Union ; I also called on E. B. Shenson, of the Relief Committee of Odd Fellows, who gave out the work and distributed the money, and while talking with him, a man came in from Detroit, and was introduced to me as Mr. Robert H. Marioni, Grand Representative of Sturgis, Michigan. I showed these two brothers my medal, and they were highly pleased with it, and said they had heard of it before, but never expected to see it. In the evening I visited Home Lodge, No. 416, and was received by the brothers in a very handsome manner.

June 5th. We all started on the Michigan Central Railroad for Detroit, and arrived there at 6 P. M. After supper we took a carriage and went through the town. Of all the places we visited in the West, the verdict of our little party was that Detroit presented more beautiful houses and better paved streets, and more beautiful sights, than any other city out West.

June 6th. Left Detroit by crossing the St. Croix River and taking cars on the Canada side for Niagara Falls.

Detroit is a splendid, clean, and beautiful city, and, should I ever want to leave my own home, I would rather go to Detroit than any place I know of, or that I have ever seen ; and this is the judgment of our whole party.

After riding around for some time, we concluded to break up our little party. Mr. and Mrs. Gregory will go right home, and Frank goes direct to Niagara Falls, and remains there until we come. My wife and self will go to my wife's brother in Canada.

This we do, and remain over night, and the next day start to meet Frank at Niagara Falls. The next day we make a final start, and arrive in Brooklyn June 13th, 1877.

"RECAPITULATION."

We left home April 3d, and arrived back home June 13th. Were gone nearly eleven weeks, and traveled during that time nearly eleven thousand miles, on cars, on stages and on horseback. We passed through 15 States, five Territories and one British Province, and they are as follows, commencing with New York, Delaware, Pennsylvania, Maryland, West Virginia, Virginia, Ohio, Indiana, Kentucky, Illinois, Wisconsin, Iowa, Nebraska, Colorado, Wyoming, Utah, Nevada, California, Michigan and Canada. And now, brothers, you who have heard this account of my trip to the West, I thank you for your kindness in listening to what I had to say. I hope you have been profited, as I have been, in telling this story of my trip to the West ; I, therefore, bid you all a good bye.

L. BOYER.